Christianity With Attitude

Giles Fraser is Team Rector of Putney in south-west London.

He is a regular columnist for the *Guardian* and the *Church Times* and a frequent broadcaster on BBC Radio 4's Thought for the Day. He was formerly lecturer in philosophy at Wadham College, Oxford.

Christianity With Attitude

Giles Fraser

CANTERBURY
PRESS
Norwich

© Giles Fraser 2007

First published in 2007 by the Canterbury Press Norwich
(a publishing imprint of Hymns Ancient & Modern Limited,
a registered charity)
13–17 Long Lane, London EC1A 9PN

www.scm-canterburypress.co.uk

Second impression 2008

British Library Cataloguing in Publication data

A catalogue record for this book is available
from the British Library

ISBN 978-1-85311-782-4

Typeset by Regent Typesetting, London
Printed in the UK by CPI William Clowes
Beccles NR34 7TL

Contents

Introduction

A few months into contributing to the *Guardian* I wrote a piece on the reaction of the National Secular Society to the tragedy of the deaths of Holly Wells and Jessica Chapman. The *Guardian* sub-editors came up with the headline: Parasites on Religion. I nearly choked on my breakfast. Letters and e-mails poured in from outraged secularists. Polly Toynbee, the grand dame of *Guardian* comment (and clearly none too pleased that she had started to share space with a vicar) used her column to denounce what I had written. Overnight, I became a pin-up hate figure for the student phalanx of Richard Dawkins's barmy army.

It's not that I minded a fight, I just felt aggrieved at being misrepresented. So I phoned up Seumas Milne, the Comment editor, to complain about a headline I thought was unnecessarily aggressive. The argument I had used in my piece was that atheism is often parasitic upon religion, in that it relies upon religion to supply the propositions that it then denies. It was, essentially, simply a point of logic. The title 'Parasites on Religion' was just way too fierce and transformed the piece into a declaration of war. Seumas' reply has remained a source of inspiration. 'I have just been reading the Epistle of James,' he said. I didn't immediately twig what he was getting at. 'Fierce, isn't it,' he observed. And that was a moment of clarity.

It was absolutely true. The Bible is fierce in its language and denunciations. The Bible doesn't hedge itself about with qualifications and hesitations. In that one observation, I recognized the failures of the rather bland and soggy language of modern Christianity, and particularly my own theological tradition of liberal Christianity. If I was going to continue writing comment pieces there was only one way forward: Christianity with attitude. Biblical writing is often fierce because the writers of the Bible, and the people they are writing about, believed in something as if their lives depended on it – and they had the honesty and bottle to say it.

Just as I had decided this was the right way forward Jeffrey John entered the storm of the Bishop of Reading debacle. My intention had always been to employ Christianity with attitude in the (mostly) loyal service of the Church of England. But this changed everything. Dr John was hung out to dry so as to placate a homophobic mob – at least, that's how I saw it. And it was the Archbishop of Canterbury – one of my personal heroes – who had his fingerprints all over the deed. He had his reasons, but I just couldn't agree with them. In the middle of the night, I sat on the stairs and thought about what I would do if I left the Church. By the morning, and after the extensive ministrations of a bleary-eyed angel in a woolly dressing gown that made a mean cup of tea, I felt strong enough to commit myself to stay. But things would never be the same again. I had been born again. Loyalty to the C of E would now have to be expressed in terms of self-criticism. Ironically, 'self-critical vigilance' is a phrase that Rowan Williams once used in an article, and I have set upon it as some sort of motto ever since.

When the Church of England tries to shut you up, it does so with the carrot rather than the stick. 'You are a talented priest, Giles. You could go far. But perhaps you ought to be a bit less angry, learn the virtues of discretion.' What a weasel word 'discretion' can often be. It comes from a family of other weasel words beloved by the Church of England – words like 'appropriate' and 'measured'. These are words that evoke a theology of those who want the C of E to be the spiritual civil service of the nation. That religion is, thankfully, almost dead. But pin-stripe Christianity isn't the real problem. The real problem is that were I to reply to the 'Giles, you are a good priest' line with anything other than a churchy version of 'bugger you' then I would have heard the cock crowing for the third time. Sometimes the Church looks considerably less morally virtuous than the rent-a-quote journalism it so enthusiastically despises.

And so I have come to find moral nobility in what is undoubtedly an arrogant and pugnacious calling. For when all is confessed about the well-canvassed failings of the modern media, journalism is really all about the search for something we used to be comfortable calling 'truth'. I can hear the snorts of derision at that word being used too closely alongside journalism. But it's that word, and that word only, that makes it a vocation capable of carrying the further description, Christian. If that sounds way too self-righteous – and I know it does – it must be immediately qualified that the fight for truth is sometimes a dirty fight. And fighting dirty for the truth may well not be a vocation capable of supporting the description Christian. Here lies the very centre of the risk of Christian comment.

I want to thank my wife, Sally, for her gentle encouragement. She doesn't have my street-fighting instincts and so is a perfect sounding board. She reads most things I write first, and has developed a very tactful vocabulary of hesitations and grimaces that has steered me away from much disaster. Thanks to Madeleine Bunting for getting me started with the *Guardian* and to Seumas Milne and all the staff on the Comment desk. My work is always immeasurably improved by their interventions. Rachel Boulding is always a star, bossing me about so delightfully at the *Church Times*. And thanks also to Christine Morgan, Amanda Hancox, David Coomes and Norman Winter from the BBC for helping shepherd me through the complexities of Thought for the Day.

And finally much gratitude to the people of St Mary's and All Saints' churches in Putney, who have been happy for their vicar to carry on with work outside the parish – something they affectionately call my 'foreign policy'. I dedicate this collection to all of them.

Chapter 1

Theology from Christmas to Easter

Happy kitschmas

The *Guardian*, 16 December 2002

Earlier this year the Catholic League of America was up in arms about an exhibition in Napa, California, which included the 'caganer', a traditional Catalan figurine who is placed squatting in the corner of the Christmas crib, trousers around his ankles. Perhaps predictably, the Catholic League was offended by the presence of a defecating peasant in the holy stable. What it didn't appreciate, however, is that the Christmas story is supposed to be offensive, and that the caganer is a reminder of the theological revolution that scandalized sophisticated opinion of the first few centuries of the Christian era: that God became human, that the sacred was no longer to be protected from the profane.

In his great masterpiece *The Unbearable Lightness of Being*, Czech novelist Milan Kundera develops an innovative moral vocabulary around the notion of kitsch. Kitsch, he argues, isn't primarily about bad taste or the vulgarities of popular devotional images: kitsch is 'the absolute denial of shit'. Kitsch is that vision of the world in which nothing unwholesome or indecent is allowed to come into view. It's the aesthetics of wanting to teach the world to sing in perfect harmony. Kitsch excludes shit in order to paint a picture of perfection, a world of purity and moral decency.

The problem with kitsch is not readily apparent because (by definition) the treatment of what is considered unwholesome takes place offstage. Think of those Nazi propaganda films of beautiful, healthy children skiing down the Bavarian Alps. Nothing wrong with that, is there? Of course there is. For this is a world that has been purified, where everything nasty or troubling has been eliminated. The logical conclusion of kitsch, argues Kundera, is the ghetto and the concentration camp – the means by which totalitarian regimes dispose of their shit, variously construed. Opening the infamous exhibition of degenerate art in the summer of 1937, Hitler gave notice that 'from now on in we will wage a war of purification against the last elements of putrefaction in our culture'. Kitsch turns out to be motivation to cleanse the world of pollution. It is the aesthetics of ethnic cleansing.

Kundera himself thinks theology to be the ultimate source of kitsch. He recounts how as a child an aimless thought experiment led him from God having a mouth to God having intestines – the implications of which struck the young Kundera as sacrilegious. This instant and visceral reaction against the association of the divine with the messiness of the human helps us appreciate something of the hostility of many early thinkers to the idea of the incarnation. God and the messiness of the world must be kept at the maximum possible distance. But what then of God become human? What of the word become flesh? Even many who felt the attraction of the Christian story believed this was going too far. Convoluted ways were sought to mitigate the offence. Christ was not really human or Christ was not really divine. Others created a firewall between the sacred and the profane within the person of Jesus himself. For the second-century Gnostic Valentinius, Jesus 'ate and drank but did not defecate'.

The Jesus of Valentinius is thus the kitsch Jesus. And it's this same kitsch Jesus of sentimental benevolence that features in countless Christmas cards and community carol services. The baby in the manger now presides over a celebration of feel-good bonhomie that makes the true meaning of Christmas almost impossible to articulate. Boozed-up partygoers and proud grandparents demand the unreality of 'O little town of Bethlehem, how still we see thee lie'. Elsewhere Kundera writes of kitsch as 'the need to gaze into the mirror and be moved to tears of gratification at one's own reflection'. And it's this gratifying reflection that many want to see when they gaze into the Christmas crib. Christmas has become unbearably self-satisfied.

The caganer is a reminder of another Jesus and another story.

From the perspective of official Christian doctrine, the story of Christmas is a full-scale attack upon the notion of kitsch. Valentinius's theology is declared heretical precisely because it denies the full reality of the incarnation. For Valentinius, Jesus only seemed human. 'Veiled in flesh the Godhead see', as the equally heretical carol puts it. Orthodoxy turns out to be vastly more radical, not because it provides a way of squaring the circle of a God-man, but because it refuses to separate the divine from material reality. God is born in a stable. The divine is re-imagined, not as existing in some pristine isolation, but among the shittiness of the world.

The temptation to disassociate the divine from material reality marks the beginnings of kitsch. For, once unhitched from the divine, the complexity of the world can be too easily by-passed and ignored. The orthodox formulation of the incarnation allows no way of avoiding politics, food, sex or money. Nor, as the Christian story of God goes on to make horribly clear, does it offer a way of avoiding suffering and death. The problem isn't that Christmas has become too materialistic – but rather that it isn't materialistic enough. Kitsch Christmas is another way of uncoupling the divine from the material, thus spiritualizing God into incapacity. I am not being a killjoy attacking the kitsch version of Christmas. On Saturday my wife gave birth to a baby boy, Felix Emmanuel. The labour ward was no place to be coy about the human body and all its functions. The talcum-powdered unreality of kitsch childbirth cannot compare with the exhaustion, pain, and joy of the real thing.

But perhaps the most important corruption of Christmas kitsch is how it shapes our understanding of peace. This is the season where the word 'peace' is ubiquitous. Written out in fancy calligraphy everywhere, 'peace and good will to all' is the subscript of the season. It's the peace of the sleeping child, peace as in 'peace and quiet', peace as a certain sort of mood. But this is not what they need in Bethlehem today. They need peace as in people not killing each other. This sort of peace requires a stubborn engagement with the brute facts of oppression and violence – which is the very reality that the kitsch peace of

Christmas wants to take us on holiday away from. How ironic: we don't want the shittiness of the world pushed at us during this season of peace. This, then, is the debilitating consequence of kitsch. Kitsch peace is the unspoken desire that war takes place out of sight and mind – it's the absolute denial of shit. Political leaders who are preparing for yet more fighting will be happy to oblige. Christmas has become a cultural danger to us all, not just a danger to orthodox Christianity.

Birth – the ultimate miracle

The *Guardian*, 20 December 2003

Why are we so obsessed with what other people think of us? Why are we so concerned to fit in? Why do we submit so readily to the tyranny of the 'they'? Heidegger's famous answer is that social conformity is a function of the fear of death. Standing alone is to face the full force of our own mortality. The crowd, on the other hand, is impersonal and immortal. The crowd is beyond the reach of death. Heidegger concludes that we hide from the unwelcome prospect of death by submerging our identity in the 'they'. The crowd anaesthetizes us from the thought of our own mortality.

The price we pay for this evasion of the grim reaper is the loss of authentic existence. Submerging our identity in the 'they', we refuse the very knowledge that individuates us and makes existence authentically our own. Death is the one thing that another cannot do on our behalf. Death gives life its quality of mineness. It is no coincidence that Frank Sinatra's rendition of 'My Way' continues to be one of the most popular requests at funerals.

During the period Heidegger was working on his philosophy of death he began an affair with a brilliant young Jewish student, Hannah Arendt. It was an extraordinary relationship. He would go on to become a celebrated apologist for the Nazi party, she would spend her life seeking to dislodge the philosophical roots of totalitarianism. Arendt learned to play dumb in his presence – pretending that 'I couldn't count up to three' – so as not to threaten the ego of the man she continued to love and forgive throughout her life. Yet despite Heidegger's philosophical celebrity, it is Arendt who offers the more important reflection upon what she regards as the pathological constellation of death and individuality.

What, she asks, if human beings were to see themselves first and foremost not as mortals but as natals? What if we were to prioritize birth rather than death in our cultural imagination? Or – to give this a seasonal twist – what if Christians were to think of the birth of Christ at Christmas as more fundamental than his death at Easter? Like all important ideas, it is both simple and brilliant.

Heidegger's thought suggests that a culture obsessed with death will place ultimate value upon self-sufficiency and subjectivity. Replacing cultural necrophilia with a celebration of birth would transform our social and political paradigms. 'Whereas mortality is the condition that leads the self to withdraw from the world into a fundamental concern with a fate that can only be its own, natality is the condition through which we immerse ourselves into the world through the goodwill and solidarity of those who nurture us,' writes Seyla Benhabib, professor of government at Yale.

The Christian story of the birth of Jesus Christ, the coming of God into the world as human, offers a number of leads to what a culture of natality might look like. St Matthew's account of the nativity begins with a long list of forebears stretching back to David and further back to Abraham. Natality emphasizes that what makes a human being unique has nothing to do with the existence of some soul-like interiority with our name stamped on it, but is established by our place within a whole network of relationships. We are authentically ourselves not in our separateness from but through our involvement with each other – an involvement we are born into. Being is communion, being is dependency.

A faith premised upon natality would have little place for an indifference to the physical. The thought that human beings are souls trapped beneath a veil of flesh makes no sense to a mother caring for her child. Likewise Plato's conception of love as an abstract intellectual virtue – that the 'beauty in souls is more honourable than that in the body' – could never have been dreamt up by someone who had given birth or spent time cuddling, kissing or tickling their kids. The love inherent within nativity is inescapably physical: beginning in the womb and continuing in the physical intimacy of feeding and cleaning.

Theologians used to worry a lot about what has been called the scandal of particularity: why did God choose to come into the world at a particular place and at a particular time? And no one has ever given a satisfactory answer – therefore the scandal. But what can and must be said is that human life is intrinsically particular. Natality insists upon particularity and refuses an abstract conception of what it is to be human. And that, for Arendt, is why a culture of natality would make totalitarianism so much more difficult to establish. For the essence of totalitarianism is the way it erases human particularity in the service of some supposedly higher cause.

Most important of all, a culture of natality would be inscribed with a permanent sense of hope. Too much Christian theology has immediately displaced this hope into the beyond, effectively denying its applicability to the world in which we live. Hence the importance of the Christian Aid strapline: 'We believe in life before death'. Often Christianity is imagined as transcending the human, in favour of some other realm, thereby betraying the constitutive elements of our humanity. But again it is Plato that is the real villain, insisting, as he does, upon transcending humanity to reach a perspective 'unalloyed, pure, unmixed, not stuffed full of human flesh and colours and lots of other mortal rubbish'. The nativity of Christ tells a very different story, returning Christians to a concern for the human in all its vulnerability and glory. In this way, a culture of natality provides a secure theological footing for an insistence upon social justice and the significance of the environment.

The western cultural imagination has been obsessed with death. No doubt, a version of Christianity that has wedded itself to Platonism is partly responsible for this unhealthy fixation. Salvation is achieved through the death of Christ. Death is the pathway to life. Properly speaking, even here it is the resurrection, the affirmation of the triumph of life over death, that is being celebrated. None the less, without the corrective of natality, a certain unhealthy morbidity can easily attach itself to the Christian vision. Even the modern rite of baptism is surprisingly heavy on the death imagery, perversely preferring a theology of death and rebirth to the miracle of birth itself. The feminist theologian Grace Jantzen, who has done most to develop a theology of natality, has suggested that the evangelical emphasis on being born again is a way in which men have wrested the power of birth away from women.

But even as Christianity recedes as a cultural influence, its patterns of belief continue to provide foundations for secular thought. As Nietzsche observed, to escape the influence of Christianity is much more complex than simply denying the existence of God. For good or ill, Christian theology continues to be inscribed within our cultural DNA, and thus the blanket refusal to think theologically can be to perpetuate the worst of the Christian tradition rather than to challenge it. That is, theology remains a public necessity rather than a strange niche market for the religious.

Empires prefer a baby and the cross to the adult Jesus

The *Guardian*, 24 December 2004

Every Sunday in church, Christians recite the Nicene Creed. 'Who for us and for our salvation came down from heaven. And was incarnate of the Holy Ghost and of the Virgin Mary and was made man; was crucified also for us under Pontius Pilate, suffered and was buried; and the third day rose again according to the Scriptures.' It's the official summary of the Christian faith but, astonishingly, it jumps straight from birth to death, apparently indifferent to what happened in between.

Nicene Christianity is the religion of Christmas and Easter, the celebration of a Jesus who is either too young or too much in agony to shock us with his revolutionary rhetoric. The adult Christ who calls his followers to renounce wealth, power and violence is passed over in favour of the gurgling baby and the screaming victim. As such, Nicene Christianity is easily conscripted into a religion of convenience, with believers worshipping a gagged and glorified saviour who has nothing to say about how we use our money or whether or not we go to war.

Christianity became the official religion of the Roman empire with the conversion of the emperor Constantine in 312, after which the Church began to back-pedal on the more radical demands of the adult Christ. The Nicene Creed was composed in 325 under the sponsorship of Constantine. It was Constantine who decided that 25 December was to be the date on which Christians were to celebrate the birth of Christ and it was Constantine who ordered the building of the Church of the Nativity at Bethlehem. Christmas – a festival completely unknown to the early Church – was invented by the Roman emperor. And from Constantine onwards, the radical Christ worshipped by the early Church would be pushed to the margins of Christian history to be replaced with the infinitely more accommodating religion of the baby and the cross.

The adult Jesus described his mission as being to 'preach good news to the poor, to proclaim release to the captives and to set at liberty those who are oppressed'. He insisted that the social outcast be loved and cared for, and that the rich have less chance of getting into heaven than a camel has of getting through the eye of a needle. Jesus set out to destroy the imprisoning obligations of debt, speaking instead of forgiveness and the redistribution of wealth. He was accused of blasphemy for attacking the religious authorities as self-serving and hypocritical.

In contrast, the Nicene religion of the baby and the cross gives us Christianity without the politics. The Posh and Becks nativity scene is the perfect tableau into which to place this Nicene baby, for like the much-lauded celebrity, this Christ is there to be gazed upon and adored – but not to be heard or heeded. In a similar vein, modern evangelical choruses offer wave upon wave of praise to the name of Jesus, but offer little political or economic content to trouble his adoring fans.

Yet despite the silence of the baby, it should be perfectly obvious to anyone who has actually read the Christmas stories that the gospel regards the incarnation as challenging the existing order. The pregnant Mary anticipates Christ's birth with some fiery political theology: God 'has brought down the powerful from their thrones and lifted up the lowly, he has filled the hungry with good things and sent the rich away empty,' she blazes. Born among farm labourers, yet worshipped by kings, Christ announces an astonishing reversal of political authority. The local imperial stooge, King Herod, is so threatened by rumours of his birth that he sends troops to Bethlehem to find the child and kill him. Herod recognized that to claim Jesus is lord and king is to say that Caesar isn't. Christ's birth is not a silent night – it's the beginning of a revolution that threatened to undermine the whole basis of Roman power.

Little wonder, then, that influential US Christian commentator Jim Wallis created a storm earlier in the year when he penned an attack upon 'Bush's theology of empire', helpfully illustrated with a picture of Bush made up to look like the emperor Constantine. 'Once there was Rome, now there is a new Rome,' argued Wallis.

Constantine was converted to Christianity by a vision that came to him on the eve of the battle of Milvian Bridge: 'He saw with his own eyes, up in the sky and resting over the sun, a cross-shaped trophy formed from light, and a text attached to it which said, "By this sign, conquer".' Soon the cross would morph from being a hated symbol of Roman brutality into the universally recognizable logo of the Holy Roman Empire. Within a century, St Augustine would develop the novel idea of just war, trimming the Church's originally pacifist message to the needs of the imperial war machine.

Like Constantine, George Bush has borrowed the language of

Christianity to support and justify his military ambition. And just like that of Constantine, the Christianity of this new Rome offers another carefully edited version of the Bible. Once again, the religion that speaks of forgiving enemies and turning the other cheek is pressed into military service.

The story of Christmas, properly understood, asserts that God is not best imagined as an all-powerful despot but as a vulnerable and pathetic child. It's a statement about the nature of divine power. But in the hands of conservative theologians, the Nicene religion of the baby and the cross is a way of distracting attention away from the teachings of Christ. It's a form of religion that concentrates on things like belief in the virgin birth while ignoring the fact that the Gospels are much more concerned about the treatment of the poor and the forgiveness of enemies.

Bush may have claimed that 'Jesus Christ changed my life', but Jesus doesn't seem to have changed his politics. As the carol reminds us: 'And man, at war with man, hears not the love song that they bring. O hush the noise, ye men of strife, and hear the angels sing.'

Hiding in silence

Church Times, 13 April 2006

No phenomenon is so widely approved of in church as silence. It suggests stillness, listening, modesty, self-examination, and gravitas. Silence is clearly holy stuff. And, because she never picks a fight with anyone, no one has a bad word to say about her. During Good Friday especially, Christians everywhere will spend hours silent before the cross. It seems the only reaction appropriate to the horror of the crucifixion.

In a brilliant essay on the representation of the Holocaust, the philosopher Gillian Rose sets her sights on the familiar idea that only silence will do in response to the horrors of Auschwitz. 'To argue for silence, prayer, the banishment equally of poetry and knowledge, in short, the witness of "ineffability", that is, non-representability, is to mystify something we dare not understand, because we fear that it may be all too understandable, all too continuous with what we are – human, all too human.' Ouch.

Rose's target is Holocaust piety. Her argument is that by enfolding us, the audience for the Holocaust, in silence, we are allowed to escape an important but profoundly disturbing realization: that we may have more in common with the perpetrators than the victims. Silence allows an unchallenged identification with the victims, which, in turn, allows a fundamental complacency to survive intact.

Silent contemplation of the unspeakable tends to lead us to tears for the victims, but not to the horrendous thought that, given different circumstances, we, too, might have been a camp guard or a Nazi thug. No one is going to admit that easily. Yet only when we face our own potential for indecency do we reach the place from which genuine change is possible.

Furthermore, those least able to recognize their own potential for wickedness are surely those most in danger of being driven by it. Those least able to see themselves as perpetrators are those who see themselves only as victims. This is why Nietzsche was right: victims are profoundly dangerous.

All of this argument is transferable to the foot of the cross. Its lesson may be something like this. Be careful, in those long silences on Good Friday, not to spend too much time in tearful identification with our Lord's suffering. Think instead of the soldiers. Become one of them. After all, it's only a job. Someone has to do it. I have my orders. Then, when you have started to put your hands on the whip and have helped hammer in the nails, only then is it the right time to break down and cry. For only then will we fully realize our desperate need for God.

The price of punishment

The *Guardian*, 31 July 2004

The language of punishment is commonly saturated with the language of finance. Criminals 'owe a debt' to society; victims seek 'compensation'; the home secretary sets a 'tariff' for various types of crime. The recent report, *Rethinking Sentencing*, unanimously approved by the Church of England General Synod, urged the Church 'to take seriously the power of the financial/economic nexus of thinking to condition responses in areas of life to which it has, in truth, no relevance'.

Yet the Judeo-Christian tradition has a good deal of responsibility for locating our thinking about punishment within a financial paradigm. Genesis describes the enslavement of Israel by the Egyptians as having been brought about by poverty. 'Now there was no food in all the land, for the famine was very severe. We with our lands will become slaves to pharaoh; just give us seed so that we may live and not die.' Salvation from slavery was primarily conceived as salvation from debt.

The Lord's Prayer, properly translated, contains the intercession, 'forgive us our debts as we forgive those who are indebted to us'. Originating here, the financial metaphor for salvation has come to be the default language for salvation. Christians speak of the remission of sins, and of Christ having paid the price of sin.

What is astonishing, however, is that the financial metaphor has flipped its meaning, and now sustains a thought process entirely at odds with the original intention. In the Hebrew Scriptures, the remission of debt was understood within the tradition of the jubilee, where all debts were wiped clean, and those in the debtors' prison of slavery released.

This tradition was invoked by the Jubilee 2000 campaign, calling for the unilateral remission of third world debt. Yet where the Hebrew Scriptures called for an intermittent use of the get-out-of-jail-free card for those endlessly imprisoned by debt, Christianity increasingly interpreted the way Christ saved humanity as 'paying back' the debt by his death on the cross.

It is a crucial difference. Whereas the jubilee tradition speaks of debts forgiven, Christ's passion is commonly understood, particularly by evangelicals, as debts paid by another on our behalf – thus protecting the reciprocity of debtor and creditor. Protecting, that is, the basic premise of finance.

This logic has more to do with Adam Smith than Adam and Eve. For the idea that sins are some sort of debt that must be paid off is to subjugate the Christian gospel of good news to the poor to the power of mammon. Penal substitutionary atonement, with its understanding of Christ as the only person 'good enough to pay the price of sin', is really all about the worship of money.

Rethinking Sentencing begins the much-needed debate into what our judicial system would look like if it was premised not on the logic of salvation as debt and repayment, but on the idea that crime is the breaking of a relationship within the community, and that genuine justice must be all about relationships restored. This is not justice as pay-back but as problem-solving. Through restorative justice, criminals are made to face the consequences of their actions and led to accept responsibility.

The prime minister has initiated the familiar auction in toughness that precedes every election. But many recognize that upping the ante against offenders is simply a diversionary exercise to satisfy the instinct for revenge. Of the 76,000 people locked up in prison in this country, many will re-offend once they have 'paid their debt'.

A genuinely biblical conception of justice that prioritizes forgiveness as a means to heal divisions is not about letting people off 'free' – that financial metaphor again – but about shifting the paradigm so that our response to crime targets the need to re-establish harmony within the community.

Easter's hawks and doves

The *Guardian*, 18 April 2003

There are two ways of understanding the theology of Easter: one is structured around the notion of retribution, the other around the notion of forgiveness. As theological literacy becomes increasingly necessary to decode what many of our world leaders are really saying, this distinction is crucial. Easter has its hawks and its doves.

The Easter of the hawks insists that sin always has to be balanced, or paid for, with pain. It's the theological equivalent of the refusal to be 'soft on crime'. From this perspective, Easter is the story of Jesus paying off the debt of human sin with his own suffering and death. As the popular Easter hymn 'There is a green hill far away' puts it: 'There was no other good enough to pay the price of sin.' Retribution is a moral necessity because through it the scales of justice are righted. Sin must be paid for with blood, just as crime must be paid for by punishment. On the cross Jesus is taking the punishment that is properly ours.

What is remarkable about this theology of debt is that it is precisely what Jesus rejects when he invokes the spirit of the jubilee at the outset of his ministry. The jubilee tradition argues for the regular unilateral remission of debt so that people are not imprisoned by a liability they cannot ever meet. It's a tradition that has been powerfully invoked in relation to third world debt, though many have little grasp of its biblical provenance. This is Jesus's good news to the poor and freedom to the captive. For the hawks, however, the spirit of the jubilee is a theological free lunch.

But the problem with the Easter of the hawks is much more than theological. The idea that human salvation is premised upon the torture and murder of an innocent life is one that has systematically weakened the capacity of European culture to set itself against cruelty. The glorification of pain and blood as the route to salvation has gone hand in hand with an obnoxious aesthetic of sadism. The 'Christian' idea that pain and guilt must be in cosmic balance has led generations of Christians to support the death penalty and oppose prison reform.

It is no coincidence that places where this sort of theology has flourished – in 17th-century England and 21st-century America – are places where justice has been, and continues to be, expressed through the scaffold or the electric chair.

From his house in South Molton Street, William Blake could see processions of the condemned making their way up Oxford Street to the gallows at Tyburn. In what Blake took to be the ultimate betrayal of Christ, the Church justified this slaughter by appealing to Christ's sufferings on the cross. Blake was characteristically fierce in his denunciation: 'Every religion that preaches vengeance for sin is the religion of the enemy and avenger and not the forgiver of sin and their God is Satan.'

Like many others before and since, Blake drew upon an alternative reading of Easter. Here the defining feature of Christ's moral teaching is an opposition to the retributive ethic encapsulated in the principle of an eye for an eye and a tooth for a tooth. Rather, Christ offered an ethic based upon forgiveness – on a refusal to become a mirror image to the violent other. In doing this he threatened to put a great deal of established religion out of business. For this established religion, based as it was on the practice of cultic sacrifice, was a way for the community to launder its own proclivity for violent reciprocity. Religion provided a safe redirection of the violent impulse and its temporary catharsis in the bloody sacrifice of small animals.

Jesus, however, takes up an alternative tradition found in the psalms and the writings of the prophets: 'I desire mercy and not sacrifice,' Jesus repeats from the book of Hosea. He thus attacks the religious authorities and is murdered for so doing. Jesus does not oppose the brutality of his treatment by an equal and opposite show of force. And in not returning violence with violence he initiates a fragile and vulnerable community of non-retaliation known as the kingdom of God. 'No future without forgiveness' is how Archbishop Desmond Tutu summed up the theology that decisively shaped the Truth and Reconciliation Commission as it sought to dismantle apartheid. The same spirit is just as necessary in taking forward the aptly named Good Friday agreement.

Despite this alternative tradition, the punitive voice of Christianity continues to exert considerable influence on public policy, not least in the US. Here a retributive doctrine of the cross is the key link between fundamentalist Christianity and right-wing politics. It's a cultural context that makes possible the question of whether torture is a legitimate means of interrogating terrorists. It's a context that encourages the belief that the tragedy of 9/11 has to be paid for with the blood of another. It's not blood for oil, as the posters say. Worse than that – it's blood for blood. This is the theology that underpins the moral convictions of the White House. And it's one Christ died opposing.

Crucified by empire

The *Guardian*, 7 February 2004

In Claude Lanzmann's harrowing Holocaust documentary *Shoah*, a Polish farm labourer is interviewed standing on the steps of her church after Sunday Mass. During the war the church had been used as a holding pen for Jews destined for the nearby death camp. Lanzmann presses her for an explanation. She answers with the story of Jesus's trial in Matthew 27. Having offered the mob a choice between Jesus and the criminal Barabbas, and the crowd having chosen Barabbas for release and Jesus for crucifixion, Pontius Pilate washes his hands of the decision. Then 'with one voice the people cried "His blood be on us and on our children"'.

Later this month, Mel Gibson's new film about the death of Christ, *The Passion*, goes on release in the United States, where it is already reopening ancient wounds. 'The film unambiguously portrays Jewish authorities and the Jewish mob as the ones responsible for the decision to crucify Jesus,' said

Abraham Foxman, director of the Anti-Defamation League after a preview screening. 'We are deeply concerned that the film, if released in its present form, could fuel the hatred, bigotry and anti-semitism that many responsible churches have worked hard to repudiate.' Rabbi Marvin Hier, founder of the Simon Wiesenthal Centre, has written to Gibson: 'For 20 centuries, the false charges of deicide and collective guilt have been the core reasons for anti-semitism, causing the death and persecution of millions of Jews.'

In 1965, as part of the reforming Second Vatican Council, the Roman Catholic Church officially rejected the blood libel of Jews as Christ killers: 'True, the Jewish authorities and those who followed their lead pressed for the death of Christ; still, what happened in His Passion cannot be charged against all Jews without distinction, then alive, nor against the Jews of today.'

Even this sounds more of a qualification than an outright denunciation of the blood libel slur – which makes it so much more disturbing that Gibson belongs to an ultra-conservative Catholic splinter organization, the Traditional Catholics, who have rejected the findings of Vatican II. While in Rome making the film, Gibson had a priest flown in from Canada to say the Tridentine Mass – the local Roman clergy apparently still tainted by the apostasy of Vatican II. Gibson's father, the single most influential figure on his theological development, described Vatican II as 'a Masonic plot backed by the Jews' and has suggested that the Holocaust was hyped out of all proportion.

Little wonder Jewish organizations are worried about the film, which opens here next month. The passion of Christ has been abused as anti-semitic propaganda for 2,000 years. At the Reformation, Protestants also got in on the act. Luther's publication of *On the Jews and their Lies* in 1543 represents one of the most disgusting anti-semitic tracts ever penned. Jews are 'our plague, our pestilence, our misfortune', they 'look into the devil's black, dark, lying behind and worship his stench'. Furthermore, 'We are at fault in not avenging all this innocent blood of our Lord. We are at fault in not slaying them. Rather we allow them to live freely in our midst despite all their murdering, cursing, blaspheming, lying, defaming.' Texts like this sent people out to kill. From the highbrow anti-semitism of successive Christian theologians to the medieval passion plays that pandered to the anti-semitism of the mob, the idea that Jews were the murderers of Christ became a bogus alibi for a violent prejudice that remains the greatest stain on the Christian character. Anything that even faintly encourages such a vision ought never to be made in celluloid.

Gibson's defence is that he is just telling it straight; that the script for the film was the New Testament itself and that it was directed by the Holy Spirit. His frustration with scholars who insist that the Gospels can't be read as neutral eyewitness biography is evident: 'They always want to dick around with it,' he complained. The pope was granted an advance screening and apparently gave it his imprimatur. 'It is as it was,' sources quoted the pope as saying – though a Vatican spokesman later denied he had made any comment. All of which begs the question: is the anti-semitism some have recognized in Gibson's film really the anti-semitism of the Gospels themselves?

Jesus was executed in a land under Roman military occupation and by the Roman authorities. Only the Romans were allowed to crucify and only the Romans had the authority to condemn a man to death. Crucifixion was a punishment for those who threatened the political status quo, not those accused of theological heresy. Of course, in first-century Palestine, as today, theology is politics. A charismatic leader who proclaimed a kingdom with God and not Caesar at its head was an immediate threat to the authorities. And as with all occupations, there were local stooges who acted on behalf of the Romans. But no one was in any doubt who was ultimately in charge. The Romans were responsible for the death of Christ.

All of which makes the story of Pontius Pilate washing his hands of the decision to execute a political/theological troublemaker entirely implausible. Brutal crowd suppression was Pilate's speciality. Governors of troublesome outposts of the Roman empire were hard-nosed career politicians who would not flinch from taking a man's life before breakfast. Can you imagine Paul Bremer sticking his head out of the hotel window and asking the Iraqi crowd whether he should send some religious agitator to Guantanamo Bay or release him?

But there is no getting away from the fact that the New Testament bristles with vociferous condemnations of 'the Jews', of Jewish leaders, Pharisees, etc. Many argue that these denunciations originate at a time of conflict between the synagogue and newly forming Christian communities that had recently been ejected from synagogue worship. On this account, the vitriol levelled against 'the Jews' is generated by a small and insecure community smarting from rejection. Moreover, given that much of the anti-Jewish rhetoric of the Gospels was written after Roman legions had returned to crush the Jewish rebellion of AD 66, some have seen the desire to blame 'the Jews' as whitewashing Roman responsibility so as not to antagonize Roman power.

What is going on here is intra-Jewish sectarian polemic. Note: intra-Jewish not anti-Jewish. The attack on 'the Jews' in the Gospels is a family argument, and is conducted with the ferocity typical of a family argument. The prophets of the Hebrew Scriptures frequently denounced Israel for failing to live up to God's expectations. 'These people draw near with their mouths and honour me with their lips, but their hearts are far from me,' insists Isaiah. Attacks upon 'the Jews' in the Gospels are of a piece with this intra-Jewish prophetic invective. But once Christianity morphed from a small Jewish sect, wrestling to establish its identity against the prevailing religious establishment, to the official religion of the Roman empire, these denunciations became deadly. Torn from the context of an intra-Jewish row for the soul of Judaism, 'the Jews' start to be heard as 'them' as opposed to 'us'. From this moment on, the Gospels are used as justification for the greatest crime in European history – the death of one Jew becoming the pretext for the murder of millions more. Christians have too often preferred an anti-semitic lie to a disturbingly relevant truth: Jesus was destroyed by the logic of empire.

The dry eyes of deep grief

The *Guardian*, 9 April 2004

In 1990 the sociologist Gillian Rose became a consultant for the Polish Commission for the Future of Auschwitz. From then until her death in 1995, she argued that the Holocaust was being narrated in such a way as to protect the present generation from the thought that they too might have something in common with the perpetrators. For Rose, the story of the Holocaust is typically told so as to place the audience alongside the victim. The crisis of glimpsing our own reflection in the face of the Nazi camp guard is a horror too far.

Thus the closing scene of the film *Schindler's List* leaves us, in her words, 'piously joining the survivors putting stones on Schindler's grave in Israel'. Despite the experience of overwhelming repulsion at the horror of Nazi genocide, too often a fundamental complacency is left unexamined. 'Instead of emerging with sentimental tears, which leave us emotionally and politically intact,' Rose said, 'we [ought to] emerge with the dry eyes of a deep grief which belongs to the recognition of our ineluctable grounding in the norms of the emotional and political culture represented.'

This week I was sent an Easter card from a group of Palestinian Christians, drawing attention to the fact that this year's anniversary of the Deir Yassin massacre falls on Good Friday. Before dawn on the morning of 9 April 1948, Jewish paramilitaries launched a surprise attack upon the quiet Palestinian village of Deir Yassin just outside Jerusalem. Soldiers went from house to house shooting old men, women and children. A group of Palestinian prisoners were paraded in trucks, taken to the local quarry, lined up and then shot.

Fahimeh Ali Mustafa Zeidan, then aged 11, described what happened: 'They blew the door down, entered and started searching the place; they got to the store room, and took us out one by one. Then they called my brother Mahmoud and shot him in our presence; and when my mother screamed and bent over my brother, carrying my little sister Khadra, who was still being breast-fed, they shot my mother too. Then they lined us up, shot at us, and left.' For the Palestinians, the massacre at Deir Yassin marks the symbolic beginning of their story of dispossession and exile.

The card goes on to make the point that 'Deir Yassin stands, unnamed and unmarked, in clear sight of the Holocaust memorial at Yad Vashem' – a reminder that the massacre at Deir Yassin occurred within three years of the liberation of Auschwitz.

There is, of course, no equivalence between Deir Yassin and the Holocaust. Furthermore, the point of comparison is badly made precisely because it is not disturbing enough. For Palestinian Christians to use Good Friday as an opportunity to reflect upon the interchangeability of victim and perpetrator ought to remind them that the passion offers Christians no comfortable space from which to be on the side of the victim.

During the liturgy of Holy Week, people who shout 'Hosanna' on Palm Sunday are the same people who shout 'Crucify' on Good Friday. The fact that the crucifixion has been the basis for centuries of anti-semitic propaganda must remind Christians – and Palestinian Christians no less so – of their own capacity for violence and brutality. The dangers of imagining oneself a weeping onlooker again leaves a fundamental complacency fully intact.

A meditation upon the shamefulness of Christian history allows Christians their most valuable insight: that there is no safe or comfortable perspective from which to stand aloof from any complicity with the horrors of the world. In my darker moments I am ashamed to be a Christian. As a Jewish Christian, I often fear that in converting to Christianity I sided with the persecutors against the persecuted. But this shame at complicity with a culture of oppression allows for a more general sensitivity to the ways we are all compromised by the endemic violence of the world. The desire to inhabit a cultural space that is unblemished is a dangerous fantasy that cooperates with the desire to avoid facing one's own capacity for brutality.

Dr Jekyll's fundamental flaw is his refusal to acknowledge the existence of Mr Hyde. Hyde can only operate in the dark, in the unexamined spaces brought about by Jekyll's pious avoidance of his own darker motivations. Rose's attack upon those narratives which place us tearfully alongside the victim is an attack upon the refusal of Jekyll to admit to Hyde. For Jekyll and Hyde are not two people but one. Tenderness, intelligence and brutality easily coexist in the same person. Our own cruelties and prejudices are given ideal conditions to grow when we refuse to admit to them.

This is not simply a meditation for the religious. For the cultural space that often has little sense of its own complicity in the horrors of the world is that of secular modernity. The new Jekyll and Hyde is the Jekyll of democratic liberalism and the Hyde of religious fanaticism. Martin Rowson's *Guardian* cartoons show those with religious belief as crazed and vicious. Good Friday is a day to admit that Christians are often guilty as charged.

But does the attack upon religious fanaticism also work in a dangerous way to excuse the secular imagination an insight into its own capacity for violence? What secular liturgies are there to reveal that those who shout 'Hosanna' are the same people who shout 'Crucify'? For the Holocaust may have taken place in a country shaped by the values of Christianity. But it took place in a country no less shaped by the values of the Enlightenment and modernity as well.

God save the Queen

Church Times, 25 February 2005

When I was a kid I used to puzzle over 'God save the Queen'. What, I wondered, did the Queen need saving from? What danger was she in? I had a mental image of a pile of bricks falling from a building site and the Queen walking by, oblivious to the masonry about to squash her. Pushing the Queen out of the way of falling bricks – now that would be saving the

Queen. But to a small kid in the pews, I couldn't work out the theological equivalent.

During Synod, the Archbishop of Canterbury warned that different traditions within the Church are in danger of completely failing to understand each other's ways of speaking about God. Indeed, such is the level of mutual incomprehension, different traditions are having trouble recognizing each other's faith as being authentically Christian. I wonder if one of the root causes of this misunderstanding is that we answer the 'saving-from-what' question in very different ways.

Here are some of the various things that theologians believe that the Queen, like the rest of us, requires saving from: sin, death, suffering, meaninglessness, error, oppression, hell, guilt, God's wrath, her enemies – and so on. The answer we choose to this question immediately suggests a very basic salvation narrative that, in turn, collects certain biblical texts, stories and metaphors around it. And the more we read and pray through our 'favourite bits' the more we come ingeniously to interpret other passages in the light of this principal narrative.

My own guiding story shifts about a bit. Sometimes it's a quasi-Girardian salvation from violence through forgiveness narrative. Other times, it's a basic exodus narrative where salvation is essentially salvation from slavery, in its various forms. This sort of theology, however, is going to look very different from that which is structured around salvation from sin. Of course, for the theologically dexterous, there are considerable overlaps, but the grain runs in different directions. On the gay debate, where many of us see oppression, others see immorality.

This isn't post-modernism, nor is this a claim that meaning is indeterminate. It is simply to say that the Bible is a collection of very different genres of texts told by different people over a great deal of time, reflecting a developing sense of what God is doing in the world. Those who seek to collapse the whole of the Bible into a single overarching story are capable of doing great violence to the text. Indeed, the belief that the Bible tells one story and one story only is the authentic hallmark of fundamentalism.

The meaning of death

The *Guardian*, 1 April 2002

Thankfully, we are learning to speak more cautiously about what is meant by victory. If ever we had any doubt, surely we now know that the war on terrorism will have no satisfying end: there will be no parades, no flag-waving, no dancing in the streets. We won't ever see a uniformed general signing the instrument of unconditional surrender.

We are also beginning to ask how the term victory could ever be applied to a situation in which so many have lost their lives and so many made homeless. As new hatreds are born from Kabul to Ramallah, we wonder if victory is anything more than a temporary pause in an exchange of violence that this current conflict has simply perpetuated. This is no armchair liberalism: it's a wisdom common even among soldiers themselves. A woman once approached the Duke of Wellington. 'A victory', she said, 'must be the most wonderful thing in the world.' The old soldier responded: 'A victory, madam, is the worst thing in the world, except only a defeat.' (NB Mr Bush and Mr Blair.) None the less, if we are asking better questions about victory, we continue to be unquestioning in our understanding of defeat.

The Jesus movement had not been going all that long before it was defeated. Some of Jesus's followers believed that here was a charismatic leader who would challenge Roman authority and re-establish a sovereign people in Israel. It didn't happen. During the busy festival period, when Jerusalem was particularly volatile, his radical message was a sufficient threat to public order for the Romans to act. He was strung up outside the city limits, pour encourager les autres. His followers scattered, dispirited and disillusioned. Realists always predicted this sort of end. Here was a man who told his friends to love their enemies and not to fight back. What else could come of such naivety?

What happened next? David Jenkins was always right: the resurrection is profoundly misunderstood if it is taken to be a conjuring trick with bones. Nor is it the case that the resurrection is the eventual success of the Jesus movement, its earlier setbacks overturned as its leader is dramatically brought back to life.

Would this be victory? Yes, it would be satisfyingly dramatic: an occasion for flag-waving and dancing in the streets. But if that were simply it, wouldn't it merely confirm the worst of our fears, that might is right – it's just that God is more powerful than the Romans. And if this is the case then nothing really has changed. My daughter learnt the following song in Sunday school: 'My God is so big, so strong and so mighty there's nothing that he cannot do.' The truth is almost the reverse of this.

The resurrection is the altered perception from which the defeat of Jesus is understood as victory. The resurrection is the vindication of peace, the perspective from which Jesus's refusal to enter into violent reciprocity is recognized as genuinely triumphant. It is the refusal of an eye for an eye or a tooth for a tooth that leads Jesus to the cross. As Simone Weil put it: 'Those who live by the sword die by the sword, and those who give up the sword die on the cross.' What the resurrection denies is the equation death equals defeat. Yes, Jesus died. No, Jesus wasn't defeated. For those still wedded to the idea of clear-cut victory this all looks suspiciously slippery.

What is there to celebrate about this sort of resurrection? The answer is that it opens up the possibility of peace, the alternative kingdom. We live in a culture hysterical about success, about winning. And yet there is no 'having-to-win' about God – that's what makes the victory of the resurrection so difficult to comprehend. From the perspective of those addicted to the old ideologies of victory and defeat, the resurrection looks like the most terrible anticlimax. Indeed, if you read the gospel stories it's hard to escape the observation that the resurrection is a bit of an anticlimax: no special effects or decisive conclusion. That sort of resurrection is a satisfying fantasy much like the satisfying fantasy of decisive military victory. Rather, resurrection accounts are disjointed, hesitant and inconclusive.

The resurrected Jesus appeared to former friends who did not recognize him. They didn't recognize him because they were looking for the wrong thing. And we continue to look for the wrong thing as we ask completely the wrong questions about the resurrection. Many Christians believe that the only important issue is whether you believe in an objective, bodily and historical event in which a person, once dead, came back to life.

What is mistaken about this is that it searches for something spectacular – and if we continue to look for that then we will never recognize him either. It's not that the resurrection is less than the objective, the bodily and the historical, but it's precisely much more than that. The resurrection is the hand of forgiveness extended to a feared other on the West Bank or Gaza Strip. It's not magic, it's the love that casts out fear.

Chapter 2

Death has lost its sting

Ash Wednesday

Thought for the Day, 2 March 2006

Lent has begun. And all over the country people have given things up – potatoes or alcohol or chocolate. There's no better time to get in shape as the weather starts to improve. And so when Easter arrives, you will be ready to enjoy the summer, fitter, happier and healthier.

What total rubbish. Yesterday, I was given the news that I am going to die. 'Know that you are dust and to dust you shall return,' said the priest, as he marked my forehead with ash. That's the message with which Lent properly begins. And that's why the Lent of cheery self-improvement is such a con. It's not about being fitter and healthier; it's about facing our own mortality. No amount of jogging will ever outpace Father Time. No cream or cosmetic can ever prevent us from becoming dust.

However obvious this is, much of our culture is intent on hiding death away and denying its reality. We used to be coy about sex, telling children they were delivered by the stork. Now we are coy about death, referring to it as having 'gone to sleep' or 'passed away'.

It's become common to spare a dying person the knowledge of their condition, so as not to upset them. We say 'everything will be all right' and 'you'll be on your feet in no time' when we know it's just not true. Often these well-meaning lies prevent important conversations from ever taking place: goodbye, sorry, I love you.

People used to die at home surrounded by their families. Now we mostly die discreetly in hospital, surrounded by machines still trying to keep us going.

It's interesting that during the middle ages the largest and most expensive building in the city would have been the cathedral. Today the largest and most expensive building in the city is the university hospital – billions of pounds of glass, steel and technology all bent on keeping us alive.

That says a lot about how our values have changed. In hospitals, doctors battle against death. Vast recourses are spent on life-saving technology. Often, behind it all is a very modern superstition – for we cannot be kept alive.

Yes, the medieval cathedral was a place of superstition too. But not about this. For when it comes to death, our ancestors were more grown up than we are. Death was an ever-present reality, not to be denied or avoided. They didn't hide it away. It prompted them to ask the big questions of human life and its purpose. What's it all about? What are we here for?

The problem with the Lent of healthy self-improvement is that it's all about avoiding these questions by living the dream of perpetual well-being. Proper Lent forces us to stop running away and face the simple truth: Know that you are dust and to dust you shall return.

Write your own obituary

Thought for the Day, 28 July 2005

NASA have calculated the probability of a fatal accident on the latest Discovery space mission as 1 in 100. Imagine what it's like to live with odds like that. The news that a small piece of protective tiling fell from the shuttle at its launch can only have increased the anxiety. It's not often explicitly mentioned, but it's clearly there behind the chewed fingernails and ashen faces: the crew undertakes this journey in the full knowledge that they are facing the possibility of their own death. It must take extraordinary courage to agree to such a mission.

But facing the reality of one's own death isn't just morbid fear – it can become something that transforms the very way we think about ourselves.

There's a spiritual exercise I undertake every year I was taught by a Jesuit friend. I compose my own obituary. Writing up the life you hope to have really focuses the mind.

First drafts are often very stupid. Giles Fraser became the Archbishop of Canterbury, he married a Danish model and played football for Chelsea. That script quickly goes in the bin. And then you start to concentrate more. What is it I really want to be? What is important? What is it I want to do with my life? It's an opportunity to think big and not be distracted by the petty projects that so commonly consume us.

And when you've written all this down, describing a life that you would be genuinely happy with, the next question is the real clincher. Are you going about your life in such a way that the story you have imagined for yourself is a real possibility? In other words, does what you want to be really connect up with who you are? It's a devastating question that can change everything. After all, no one's written the obituary for you. And so, asking yourself if you're really going to become this person is simply facing the truth about who you really want to be.

Part of what makes the New Testament so focused a work of moral imagination is that it was written under the belief that the end of the world was drawing close. It was written with a huge sense of impending danger that created a form of concentration that burnt away the trivial. Facing the end puts all things into perspective.

When bombs went off in central London, my first thought was for the safety and whereabouts of my family. I was instantly reminded of what I really love and care for, what's important. It's all too easy to trundle through life without properly taking stock, focusing instead on domestic worries about the mortgage or the next promotion at work. Real danger can come as a wake-up call for the unreflective life.

Dying to live

The *Guardian*, 10 January 2003

Beneath the question of whether a nutty sect has actually cloned a baby lies the more interesting question of why it wants to. 'The goal is to give humans eternal life through cloning,' say the Raelians. It is supposed to work like this: you make a clone copy of me and then 'download' my personality into the clone. The clone thus becomes a revitalized version of me. And you can keep on doing this, making copies of the copy, ad infinitum. Hence I live for ever.

The reason this is rubbish has nothing to do with the capabilities of science. It's rather a question of what makes me me – what philosophers call the question of personal identity. The Raelians presume that an accurate copy of me, a copy that shares the same DNA, is the same thing as me. But it just isn't.

Part of the dodge that makes the cloning idea look half plausible is that we are led to imagine the clone taking on the parent's downloaded personality at the time of the parent's death. In this way the parent and the clone are not thought of together in the same space, but rather as one succeeding the other, the 'I' being handed down the generations. But what if we imagine the parent's personality being downloaded into a clone, or even multiple clones, which then live alongside the parent. Can we really make sense of the idea that there are actually half a dozen people, all living at the same time, all of whom are really me? We don't treat identical twins as one person, so why should we treat my identical clone and me as one person?

One of the ways we can test whether it is nonsense to speak of clones with identical downloaded personalities as being the same person as the originating self is when we think about questions of responsibility.

Imagine, after I die, it is discovered that I had committed a terrible murder. Would my clone then be responsible? Would it be right to send him to prison? At the trial my clone would protest that it wasn't him but his parent who committed the crime. And he would be right – the conclusion of which is that whatever the physical and psychological similarities between clone and parent, the two can never be the same person. If this is the case then there can be no eternal life through cloning; simply, at best, a succession of different people who happen to look and behave the same way as me. What a nightmare.

But even if it were possible to live for ever, would we really want to? And would human life really be as valuable if we were able to do away with the limits that define it? American philosopher Martha Nussbaum makes the point that it is the limitations of being human, in particular the limitation of our mortality, that gives meaning to what we are and much that we value. Indeed, a life that is without the possibility of death seems altogether more shallow in comparison.

In classical literature much is made of gods who fall in love with mortals. The beautiful goddess Calypso offers Odysseus a life on her island free from ageing and death. But rather than accept her offer of immortality Odysseus chooses to continue his dangerous journey, a journey fraught with risk and the possibility (and eventual certainty) of death, so that he might come again to his beloved Penelope.

In the world of the immortal ones there can be no such thing as risking one's life for the love of another. There can be no room for the heroism of sacrifice. No wonder the gods fall in love with mortals, for compared to the anaemic possibilities of immortal love the love of mortals is always going to be more passionate and intense. What, for example, becomes of the desire to protect and nurture another when welfare is guaranteed in advance? What sense can there be in the anxious and loving attention one pays to a fragile human baby if human life is invulnerable?

Advances in biotechnology and medicine are constantly pushing back the limits of our mortality, helping us live ever longer lives. It's one thing to push against the limits, it's another thing entirely to imagine human life without any such limits. For it is our fragility that makes us what we are. And as Nietzsche argued against Christianity, the fantasy of never-ending life, of life without fragility, is not a celebration of the human but a disparagement of it.

But Nietzsche misunderstood Christianity on this point. For the aim of Christianity, as well as that of most of the world's mainstream religious traditions, isn't about living for ever: it's rather about the transfer of interest from self to God. 'We must divest ourselves of the idea that limitation implies something derogatory or even a kind of curse or affliction,' argued Swiss theologian Karl Barth. Rather, Christianity speaks of dying to self. What this involves is wholly incompatible with the ego's obsessive desire to go on and on. For eternal life isn't living for ever: it's a freedom that begins the other side of self-regard.

Estranged from death

The *Guardian*, 10 May 2002

The new University College Hospital trust building, £420m of glass and steel, has been described as a 21st-century answer to cathedrals. It's an interesting comparison, for like the great medieval cathedrals, the magnificence of university hospital buildings, so evident particularly in the US, reveals a great deal about the hopes and fears of the societies that built them. They also say much about the attitudes of their respective communities to death and dying.

According to the book of Ecclesiastes: 'For everything there is a season, and a time for everything under heaven, a time to be born and a time to die.' But when is the right time to die? We used to have a sense of these things: three score years and ten was the shorthand. It was a time-span made sense of by the rhythms and responsibilities of community life. Shakespeare wrote of the seven ages of man. But the idea of having 'a good death' makes little sense to us now, for the expectations of how long we live are no longer related to patterns of community life, or to a sense of our responsibilities discharged, but to the state of medical technology – very expensive medical technology celebrated in glass and steel. We now die when the medics have failed us, when the doctor cannot do anything more. We no longer share a sense of what a natural life-span might be or of any appropriate time for our life to come to an end.

This lack of public consensus could open an enormous economic black hole. For if there is no sense of an appropriate end to human life, then there is potentially no end to the resources we ought to commit to extending it. Some scientists now tell us that there is no reason, in theory, why we cannot extend our lives indefinitely. This may be more science fiction than science, but, just like science fiction itself, it tells us much more about the present than it does about the future. The Queen Mum lives to 102 and all our life-span expectations are imperceptibly raised. Is it now 'premature' to die in one's 80s? I don't think we know.

And worse, I don't think we are in possession of the emotional and political maturity for proper debate on the subject. The language of individual rights surely won't help us either, for what we need here is a language that attempts to understand what human life is for. It's a language we are no longer very good at speaking. Yet it's a language we must develop in considering the proper allocation of resources within the NHS.

The first stage in this debate must be to recognize the unrealistic expectations that are loaded into our popular conceptions of medicine. For medicine remains the one area of contemporary life still affected by the Enlightenment dream that a combination of science, reason and human ingenuity can make all things possible. Indeed, these great glass and steel hospitals are surely a reflection of the great hubris of the Enlightenment and of its belief in the power of progress. No surprise these buildings look like multinational corporate headquarters, for the capitalist machismo of their architecture is a natural complement to the state of contemporary medical science. But hubris has a price, for the dream of unfettered scientific progress combined with a lack of any sense that human life has a natural or appropriate end is a recipe for economic disaster. It's a recipe for emotional disaster too, for no longer having any idea of what a 'good death' might mean, we become increasingly dyslexic in our articulation of grief or fear. This incapacity breeds multiple superstitions about death and all sorts of fearful fantasies about its processes. If all we ever do is try desperately to keep death at bay, at any price, it is inevitable we become hysterical about it.

Priority in health service resource allocation must be given to the care of patients (not clients or consumers). It's beds in the corridors and horrendous waiting lists we need to tackle, rather than spending money on expensive innovative technologies that search for ever more ingenious ways of keeping us alive. In fact, it's an ancient wisdom we need to recover. In the 5th century St Benedict shaped the future of monasticism by arguing that every guest, whatever their condition, must be treated and cared for as one might care for Christ. Monasteries set aside spaces for the care of their guests and the hospital was born, the word 'hospital' deriving from the Latin for 'guest'. Hospitals were originally places of hospitality. The hospice movement is the nearest contemporary equivalent, understanding that the advances in medical science must not be seen as an end in themselves, but ought to be subservient to the care of their guests. It is a part of what can make hospices such wonderfully life-affirming places. And that's precisely what we now need in the NHS.

On giving up smoking

Thought for the Day, 2 September 2004

The battle against smoking continues. Scotland's first minister Jack McConnell has just returned from Ireland to review the effect of the Irish ban on smoking in public places. 'I am now closer to the idea that a consistent ban would be advantageous,' he said. Elsewhere, the Greencroft School in County Durham has been making the news for giving out nicotine patches to children as young as 14.

But for all the government initiatives and programmes, giving up smoking is necessarily a singular business, a matter of individual conversion, so to speak. It's been five weeks since my last cigarette, and since then I have been wrestling with demons. Trying to give up, I dream about smoking. I wake up in cold sweats. In times of stress I think of cigarettes as friends who carry and support me. I love them and they love me. Except I don't love them – I hate them. Like Gollum, I speak to myself in two voices.

What a perfect metaphor for what we used to be comfortable calling sin. The voice of my tempter goes like this: 'Focus on the craving. Can you feel the emptiness? And just think, with one cigarette, all those swirling emotional and physiological needs will be satisfied. Relief will be instant.' But far from defeating the craving, relief is constantly deferred, the site of supposed satisfaction is the place for yet further desire – desire for something that remains cruelly forever out of reach. St Paul describes sin as a power to which one has become enslaved – and that's just what it feels like.

But not only do the demons of addiction crawl all over my need, they also lead me into great clouds of self-deception. Consider the following, all of which I have believed at one time or another. (1) I will not be able to think or write properly without a cigarette. (2) I like smoking because I like the idea of being a bit of a rebel. (3) Smoking makes me more approachable as a vicar. (4) Smoking is so bound up with my identity that if I give it up I will no longer be me. Sad, isn't it. My demons tell me that without cigarettes I won't be clever, cool or confident.

The battle with cigarettes is one that is played out in the desert spaces of my imagination. And like many of the great spiritual battles of the soul, it involves staring into the face of death. It was ten years ago today that Roy Castle died of passive smoking. On hospital wards the length of the country, hundreds more will die again today. To misquote St Paul: the wages of smoking is death.

Remembrance Sunday

Thought for the Day, 12 November 2005

Last year, for the first time, and I very much hope for the last, I had the experience of being shot at. The crack of semi-automatic gunfire, the telltale puffs of dust as bullets impacted the ground: this was not the sort of eventuality they prepared me for at vicar's training college. And I didn't conduct myself with any great distinction. In a moment of thoughtless panic, I ran for cover. I did not turn to see if others were OK. I just ran.

Thank God, no one was hurt more than cuts and bruises. Nonetheless, that disturbing afternoon in Gaza often revisits me in dreams. Which may be why I recently picked up the sort of book I'd normally never read: General Sir Peter de la Billiere's *Supreme Courage*, an anthology of stories of those who have won the Victoria Cross for valour.

I haven't much time for the boy's-own fantasy of courage that pretends it's possible to be without fear. I wanted to know what made for the real thing. What enables somebody to walk out into a hail of bullets, knowing that they may never come back?

Peter de la Billiere explains it thus: 'Each of us has a bank of courage. Some have a significant credit balance, others little or nothing; but in war we are all able to make the balance last longer if we have' – and here's an interesting list – 'training, discipline, patriotism and faith.' These are not words that resonate very strongly with the rock 'n' roll generation into which I was born. Like the word 'duty', these words can come across as cold and authoritarian. But to see them this way is profoundly to misunderstand them.

Captain Noel Chavase, a medic in the Liverpool Scottish regiment and son of the Bishop of Liverpool, was twice awarded the VC during the First World War for rescuing the wounded in no man's land. Letters back to his girlfriend made me cry. He would never enjoy that happy settled life of which he dreamed. Instead, he bled to death at Passchendaele among the squalor of the trenches, still fighting to save others.

Why on earth would he do this? Why would he risk every-thing for strangers? Because, I guess, he was captivated by a sense of how the world ought to be that became more important to him than he was to himself. Duty meant a hard and practical commitment to the belief that the world should be different: just, free and peaceful.

And while many have this commitment without religion, there is no doubt that a belief in something worth defending with one's life, a belief in something far greater than oneself, takes one into the hinterlands of religious faith. 'Greater love hath no man than this, that he would lay down his life for his friends.'

Morality and war

Church Times, 13 January 2006

I'm off to lecture on the intermediate command and staff course at the Defence Academy in Shrivenham this week. The prospect of talking to more than 400 newly promoted majors from the army and marines about the moral dimensions of conflict has got me biting my nails and poring over Carl von Clausewitz's classic study *On War*.

Von Clausewitz would think my lecture absurd. 'We can never introduce a modifying principle into the philosophy of war without committing an absurdity,' he argues. The logic of war is such that it makes no sense to speak of moral constraints on warfare. Indeed, 'The ruthless user of force who shrinks from no amount of bloodshed must gain advantage if his opponent does not do the same.'

It's a chilling philosophy that has enough truth to it to be taken very seriously. Is a 'moral soldier' at a disadvantage in the field of battle? Shying away from 'doing whatever it takes', is a moral soldier more likely to be killed, and to get his comrades killed?

I wonder whether part of the problem is that ethics is too often presented in terms of limits, as if the essence of a moral formulation is 'thou shalt not . . .' If this is so, soldiers may well think of *jus in bello* as fighting with one hand tied behind their backs. Consequently, they may nod in the direction of ethics, but deep down think of ethics as a civilian luxury that doesn't travel well to places such as Basra.

Surely the answer must be something like this: if a war is ever to be counted just, it must be fought to protect or liberate – fought to bring about some positive moral vision. In the case of Iraq, it's supposed to be democracy and freedom for Iraqis, and greater security and stability for their neighbours.

Those who fight have a responsibility to that vision, not least because it would be – to use von Clausewitz's word – absurd to fight in the name of a better world with actions and methods that corrode that vision. That is why it is absurd for George Bush to claim the war in Iraq is about human rights, while torturing prisoners and holding them in secret prisons for years without trial.

Ethics is not fundamentally about restrictions: it is about a positive vision. Moral restrictions derive from that. As the *Miami Herald* put it recently after a blistering attack on President Bush's war: 'Ultimately, our best defence against attack – any attack, of any sort – is holding fast and fearlessly to the ideals upon which this nation was built.' It sounds counter-intuitive, but ethics is not a danger to soldiers. On the contrary, in a country such as this, it can be the only purpose of soldiers' existence.

God is not the puppet master

The *Guardian*, 8 January 2005

Churches are usually packed for the funeral of a baby. But this funeral had just four mourners: the baby's young mother, her

42

best friend, and the baby's two sisters. For whatever reason, there was no wider circle of family and friends to offer emotional support. The tiny coffin was dwarfed by the freezing cold emptiness of my Anglo-Catholic church. Blood ran down the mother's arm. In utter desperation she had scored the name of the child into her arm with a knife just before the service.

That night, and for some weeks after, I lost my faith. Oxford theology hadn't prepared me for the realities of parish life in the Black Country. I thought of W. H. Auden: 'Was it to meet such grinning evidence we left our richly odoured ignorance. Was the triumphant answer to be this? The pilgrim way has led to the abyss.'

Since then, I have sat through endless undergraduate tutorials on the so-called 'problem of evil'. If God is all-powerful and all-loving, how can suffering exist? The essays that are most difficult to stomach are those that seek some clever logical trick to get God off the hook, as if the cries of human suffering could be treated like a fascinating philosophical Rubik's cube in need of an ingenious solution. Such 'solutions' include: the universe is set up like some cosmic Gordonstoun where suffering makes us better people. Or – without suffering the world would become some sort of toy world where nothing has moral weight. Or – (believe it or not) devils are responsible, not God. Of course, none of them works, and one has to question the moral health of those whose only concern in the face of great tragedy is to buy God some dubious alibi.

So why am I still a Christian? Because, in part, the intellectual problem of suffering does not accurately depict the reality of human pain and how we respond to it. It is significant that in more than ten years of being a priest, of taking heartbreaking funerals and of being face to face with much human tragedy, no one has seen fit to ask me how God and suffering can coexist. Yes, there is the burning question 'why?' – and sometimes it's spat out with great bitterness – but it's not a tutorial-type question as much as a cry of deep despair. This is not the sort of suffering that can be traded as an intellectual commodity in some wider game of atheist versus believer. And far from being a reason for people to take their leave of God, many find that the language of God is the only language sufficient to express their pain and grief, even rage.

As Rowan Williams put it, quoting one of his predecessors as Archbishop of Wales who had himself lost a child: 'All I know is that the words in my Bible about God's promise to be alongside us have never lost their meaning for me. And now we have to work in God's name for the future.'

But this does not offer the Christian worldview unlimited protection from the stormy blast of the tsunami. Christians cannot go on speaking about prayer as if it were an alternative way of getting things done in the world, or about divine power as if God were the puppet master of the universe. What is so terrifying about the Christmas story is that it offers us nothing but the protection of a vulnerable baby, of a God so pathetic that we need to protect him. The idea of an omnipotent God who can calm the sea and defeat our enemies turns out to be a part of that great fantasy of power that has corrupted the Christian imagination for centuries. Instead, Christians are called to recognize that the essence of the divine being is not power but compassion and love. And it's this love, and this love only, that whispers to me in defiance of the darkness: all will be well, all manner of things will be well.

Chapter 3

The bloody Church

Committee-shaped Church

Church Times, 3 March 2006

More bits of paper come through the door containing election material for loads more General Synod committees. My heart groans. We are not a mission-shaped Church. We are a committee-shaped Church, run by committee people for committee people.

Once committees get established, they are self-propagating. People who put themselves forward for them are generally those who think committees are a good thing. So committees self-select in favour of those who work in a particular way. As every new challenge emerges, the committee invariably sees yet another committee as the answer.

Like ground elder, once the committee system has taken root, it's a devil of a job to get rid of it. It grows and spreads and chokes the life out of the other plants in the garden. The nightmare of the committee-shaped Church is that we end up with all the energy and charisma of a call centre in Slough – a vision of the kingdom being replaced by a discussion of last month's minutes.

Back in the mid-part of the 20th century, philosophers such as Theodore Adorno were warning about the changes to society that were being brought about by the extension of bureaucracy. He argued that, in the wake of the Enlightenment, social policy came to be dominated by a way of thinking characterized by evaluation, measurement, and testing. In this efficient style of thinking, subjectivity is steadily eradicated.

As he put it: 'Thinking objectifies itself to become an automatic, self-activating process – an impersonation of the machine that it produces itself so that ultimately the machine can replace it.'

One of the important aspects of Adorno's vision is his claim that such systems of thought are good at 'means-and-ends' questions, but unable to answer (or even ask) 'why' questions. Indeed, he argues, it was precisely this emphasis on efficiency – yet the failure to question why – that created blindness in thousands of Germans who worked towards the establishment of the Nazi death camps.

The committee-shaped Church is also good at blocking out questions of the wrong shape, and focusing instead on efficiency and management. It is so ironic. One of Adorno's observations is that this style of thought is peculiarly secular, a consequence of the universe's becoming cold, technical, and disenchanted. No wonder there is clergy burn-out. We thought we were reaching for the kingdom. Years later, we realize we are working for just another multinational conglomerate.

Dialectical Anglicanism

The *Guardian*, 17 June 2006

The Church of England is currently being tortured by a dead German philosopher. An unlikely story, I know. But not when you recall that the head of the Anglican Church is a former Oxford don with a deep love of Hegel. And it's partly because of Hegel – specifically Rowan Williams's commitment to Hegelian dialectics – that morale in the Church of England is so low.

For those who didn't spend hours in the student bar plotting the overthrow of global capitalism, it may be worth a recap. The dialectic proposes that human culture advances through a serious of oppositions. A thesis is opposed by its opposite, an antithesis, which is then taken up into a synthesis of the two, shifting culture into a whole new territory. Here is Dr Williams's explanation: 'Reflection requires that the plain opposition of positive and negative be left behind. Thinking is not content with the abstraction of mutual exclusivities, but struggles to conceive of a structured wholeness nuanced enough to contain what appeared to be contradictories.'

The Canterbury dialectic was in evidence at a summit of bishops who were considering whether they should remain a boys' club. It works like this. Take someone who believes that women ought to be bishops. Take someone who believes women ought not to be bishops. Put them in a room with flip-charts and shake them all about, and you come out with a synthesis. Or a structured wholeness nuanced enough to contain what appeared to be contradictories. But you don't. What really happens is that you come up with a bodge and a room full of very angry Christians, exhausted by the politics of eternal negotiation.

Following Hegel, the archbishop believes that all oppositions can be nuanced into resolution. It's a matter of faith for him. The dialectic describes the path a divided humanity must travel if it is to reach the good infinity, the kingdom of heaven. It's the way of personal and social transformation under which all human conflict will come to an end. The lion will lie down with the lamb.

Long before Hegel drew breath, Anglicanism has always had something of Hegel about it. After all, the genius of the Church of England is to create a synthesis of Catholics (thesis) and Puritans (antithesis). But whereas historic Anglicanism believed that compromise between different theologies was a price worth paying for a truce between them, Dr Williams's dialectical Anglicanism is an encouragement to war.

For dialectical Anglicanism just cannot say no. Every no always comes with its attendant yes. And that means, it can't resist the bigotry, sexism and homophobia that is currently making a nasty comeback in the Anglican pulpit. Whether it be those who would treat women clergy as second class or those who compare gay Christians to beasts, the logic of Dr Williams's position is always to accommodate. Commendably inclusive, some presume. But this sort of inclusivity offers little protection against those who would undermine the tolerance that has been the Anglican trademark. When dealing with well-organized and well-motivated bullies, it's a hopeless philosophy.

49

Worse still, the dialectical quest for unity is callously indifferent to the casualties of its grand plan. Isaiah Berlin was right to call the dialectic 'a sinister mythology which authorizes the infinite sacrifice of individuals to such abstractions as states, traditions or the destiny of the nation' – or, one might add, to the unity of the Church. Even Hegel admitted that the dialectic is a 'slaughter-bench' on which the welfare of individuals is counted as collateral damage. Isn't that precisely what happened to Jeffrey John?

But the saddest casualty of Hegel's system of reconciliation is the archbishop himself. Holding all these opposites in tension is grinding him down. He presents as Christ on the cross, taking upon himself the pain of the Church's division. Each new fight is a spear in the side, yet he continues to maintain faith in the reconciling process of nuance. If he's right, it's a work of supreme Christian sacrifice. If he's wrong, all this pain will have been for nothing.

The end of the country vicar

The *Guardian*, 13 April 2006

There was a time when the country vicar was a staple of the English dramatis personae. This tea-drinking, gentle eccentric, with his polished shoes and kindly manners, represented a type of religion that didn't make non-religious people uncomfortable. He wouldn't break into an existential sweat or press you against a wall to ask if you were saved, still less launch crusades from the pulpit or plant roadside bombs in the name of some higher power.

Safe though he was, the nice country vicar in effect inoculated vast swathes of the English against Christianity. A religion of hospital visiting and flower arranging, with a side offering of heritage conservation, replaced the risk-all faith of a man who asked his adherents to take up their cross and follow him. The nice country vicar represented a very English modus vivendi between the sacred and the secular, with the sacred, in swallowing many of its convictions, paying by far the heaviest price for the deal.

In exchange for a walk-on part during major family occasions and the opportunity to be custodian of the country's most impressive collection of buildings, the vicar promised discretion in all things pertaining to faith: he agreed to treat God as a private matter. In a country exhausted by wars about religion, the creation of the non-religious priest was a masterstroke of English inventiveness. And once the priest had been cut off from the source of his fire and reassigned to judge marrows at the village fête, his transformation from figure of fear to figure of fun was complete.

The same genius at containing the power of religion was at work in the establishment of the Church of England. Secularists think this arrangement gives the Church too much influence over the state, but it's the other way round: it secularizes the Church. When Puritan settlers in America set up a firewall between Church and state, it wasn't to protect the state from the Church, but to protect their Church from the state. And comparing England and the US, it would seem – however counter-intuitive – that it's precisely this separation that allows the American churches more influence over their government. Establishment domesticates the potentially dangerous enthusiasm of religion so that we might be 'quietly governed'.

It's not simply that the English sought to quarantine God so as to eliminate him. Take choral evensong. Safe in the knowledge that proceedings will be ordered, beautiful and modest, the English are happy enough to creep in at the back of the church and allow their spirits to take flight on the back of an anthem by Stanford or Howells. In England, even God succumbs to principles of good housekeeping: 'a place for everything and everything in its place'.

The country vicar, the established Church, choral evensong – they represented threads of a complex settlement that developed over centuries between Christianity and the English. No one has yet worked out the consequences of this settlement having come to an end. But come to an end it most certainly has. The country vicar is a dying breed, his natural habitat slowly eroded as villages become pretty dormitories for people who work in towns. Economics did for the village shop and the pub – and they may well do for the traditional country church too. The only reason disestablishment doesn't stand a chance is that no government will ever assign it the vast amount of parliamentary time that would be required. And only tourists go to choral evensong these days.

Many people confuse these changes with the declining influence of religion. In fact religion has returned to top of the agenda. Indeed, it was resurgent religion that delivered the coup de grace to the doctrinally inert country vicar. Belief is now back, often red in tooth and claw. In the minds of many, God is about terrorism, hatred and gay-bashing. And the ghost of the country vicar looks on with puzzled anguish. As Yeats put it: 'The best lack all conviction, while the worst are full of passionate intensity.' The challenge for today's Church is to prove Yeats wrong. Liberals need to rediscover their fight and evangelicals need to learn that there is much in religious belief that is right and proper to fear.

On Good Friday, Christians remember the crucifixion. Those who welcomed Christ into Jerusalem on Palm Sunday now bay for his blood. Even the hard-nosed career soldier Pontius Pilate fears the passionate intensity of the mob. As day falls, God is butchered on a cross. There's no way of doing theological justice to any of this without breaking into a serious existential sweat. And that's why the central-casting country vicar just didn't add up. But the intense energy of Good Friday is easily purloined for hysterical and destructive purposes. One only has to think of the ways the story of the cross has been used to fuel centuries of anti-semitism. The life of faith has to come with a public health warning: religion can kill.

We are currently witnessing the slow break-up of the last great nationalized industry: the Church of England. And these changing circumstances require a new settlement. As a public body, the English Church became mired in procedure, pomp and bureaucracy. It failed to live up to the daring energy and enthusiasm of its founding message.

Even the Archbishop of Canterbury is now calling for a new order: 'A lot of the training of clergy has tended to prepare for maintenance rather than expansion, or even sometimes for managing decline. We've got to find new ways of encouraging the sort of ministry that will be prepared to be entrepreneurial, that will take risks, that will step outside the conventional patterns, the conventional boundaries of the way church is done.'

The new buzz in the C of E is towards a free market in religious expression. Still frustratingly cautious, none the less these fresh expressions of Church suggest a religion without the checks and balances provided by the traditional English settlement. What's being imagined is a more energetic and vigorous Church. And if the transformation to an entrepreneurial model is followed through, it will undoubtedly see many more people coming to church. But it will also see religion conducted beyond the hesitancy for which the old Church of England has always been known. And that will make it unstable and unpredictable. As the old order breaks apart, the worry is that we may release the genie of English religious fanaticism from the establishment box in which it has been dormant for centuries.

Walk the walk, junk the junk

Church Times, 21 May 2004

One of the besetting curses of church life is clutter. The three kings brought gold, frankincense and myrrh: the lovely Mrs Miggins brings empty jam-jars, dog-eared tracts on spirituality, and a half-broken chair that 'might be useful to somebody, some day'.

Things like this pile up in the dusty corners of the building, nobody quite knowing who has the authority to throw them out. This uncertainty transforms the side aisle into a store for junk. Regular churchgoers get used to it. Newcomers notice immediately.

The caricature clergyperson is an inveterate hoarder. Chuckers like me are deemed wasteful. The recycling movement has given those whose thrift was schooled during the war years a new justification for piling up junk. But responsible stewardship of the planet's resources does not mean the church should store those things that didn't sell in the car boot sale.

This sympathy towards clutter is symptomatic of a reluctance to address the management of resources. Those who fail to notice the cluttered aisle also fail to notice the cluttered bureaucracy of the Church. Damp and dusty churches that attract half a dozen worshippers are kept alive on the drip of centralized subsidies that lock problems in place.

My burgeoning ecclesiastical Thatcherism is heresy outside evangelical churches – but the evangelicals are correct. Without the discipline imposed by financial reality, shrinking churches are offered little incentive to change. Yes, richer churches must support poorer ones, and sacrificially so. No, redistribution of wealth must not be contingent on theology. But we need urgently to transform church culture and encourage initiative.

Twenty-five years after the start of the Thatcher revolution, the Church of England remains the one nationalized industry untouched by her insistence that there is a link between bureaucracy and waste. At the time, I couldn't see what she was doing as anything other than an attack on the vulnerable. But after a decade of ministry in the Church of England, I begin to appreciate that the energy of the entrepreneur is thwarted by layers of convoluted committees and form-filling.

A mission-shaped Church must address these systemic issues, whatever the pain. Nationalized industries are good at offering universal service-provision (excuse the pun), but poor at transforming themselves into something proactive. Unless we meet this challenge, our churches will become carpet warehouses or tourist attractions.

They throw themselves at me

Church Times, 20 August 2004

Some churches set out to woo new members with all the charisma of spotty adolescents combing the pub for super-models. There is little more unattractive than the combination of desperation and corny chat-up lines. This, for example, is the effect of the unspeakably awful 'CH__CH: what's missing? UR', and the like.

The chatting-up analogy is more than flippancy. If I remember the painful days when the search for Mrs Fraser was at the top of the psychological agenda, there were two golden rules, learnt from much embarrassment and disappointment.

First, there is no such thing as a good chat-up line. The idea that you could begin to win somebody's heart with the witticism of a Christmas cracker joke is pathetically stupid, patronizing to the object of your attentions, and demeaning to yourself. The same is true of seeking to attract those who would give their heart to Jesus.

Furthermore, the clumsy evangelistic chat-up line has a corrosive effect on the reputation of the Church in general. We are the people of God, called to take up our crosses and follow Christ. One cannot be called into such a life of commitment with the moral seriousness of an advert for a lollipop.

The second golden rule is that you are more likely to meet Mr or Miss Right when you are not actively looking for him/her. I suppose this is another way of saying that people find you more attractive when you are yourself and not pretending to be something else.

Declining church attendance can lead to a loss of confidence and the unmistakable whiff of desperation, as I have found in the responses to the new Grove booklet, *Creating a Culture of Welcome* by Alison Gilchrist. In this context, the fact that you have WELCOME in fancy lettering on your church noticeboard might say something completely different from what you think it does; something my older daughter might recognize as 'sad'.

Our confidence is rooted in something deeper, and we need to show that in how we present ourselves.

Still, gentle guile can sometimes work a treat. I often have conversations that go like this: 'You're a bit different/fun/lively. I can't believe you are a vicar. I might come along to your church . . .' The tone is of someone doing me a huge favour.

My response is often something like this: 'We'd love to see you, of course. But we are often very busy, and space is limited.' More often than not, they are there next Sunday. Sometimes it's worth playing hard to get.

Top of the Pops: good riddance

Church Times, 4 August 2006

Top of the Pops – RIP. After 42 years, the BBC's flagship pop-music TV show has breathed its last. Good riddance, I say. Even as a kid, I hated it. And I will be forever grateful to my children's generation for seeing through its fakery, and switching over to MTV.

The case against TOTP is simple: in the search for the permanently cheerful, it came to represent popular culture as glib and trivial. With its excruciatingly upbeat presenters such as Jimmy Savile and Noel Edmonds, TOTP demanded a lack of seriousness from its musical content. Everything had to be poptastic.

I am exactly the same age as TOTP; we grew up together. As I fought my way through the emotionally complex thicket of adolescence, my moral sensibilities were shaped by bands such as The Jam and The Clash. They were angry, politically engaged, and musically sharp. In thousands of teenage bedrooms, a generation would sing along: 'Time is short and life is cruel – but it's up to us to change This town called malice.' It's easy to smirk at the over-earnestness of the morally superior adolescent. But this was how many of us first tried out the language of right and wrong.

But, while all this was going on, the irritatingly smug TOTP came to portray the interests of the young as forever bent towards smiley ephemeral nonsense. That's why it was always wonderful to see some performers refusing to mime along to the soundtrack of their songs, thus exposing the format of the show as a sham. TOTP was essentially an adult's view of what young people are like. And those musicians who became TOTP saboteurs seemed to be striking a blow against a definition of youth culture decided by supposedly trendy adults.

Unfortunately, the whole poptastic spirit still lives on, often in church. Indeed, there is nothing quite as nauseating as middle-aged church leaders trying to do youth worship, and projecting on to young people a whole set of assumptions that say more about the middle-aged than the young. My heart sinks when I hear yet another Christian leader speaking of being relevant (ahhh!) to young people, and meaning by this the proclamation of a poptastic gospel.

If the Church is to retain any credibility with the young, it must stop making itself look so culturally clumsy by trying desperately to ape youth culture. What the young are able to spot very quickly is that a great deal of youth worship, like TOTP, is really all about sad adults trying to recapture their youth.

Dealing with people who stop mission

Church Times, 28 April 2006

Here's an uncomfortable truth: a large number of people in the pews do not share the enthusiasm for mission that is necessary to save the Church. Though most pay lip-service to the priority of mission, many in reality prefer their own church to remain small. It's especially true of people who have gone to a particular church for years. They have got things organized. The problem with new people is that they want to do things differently.

An emphasis on pastoral care for a congregation should not inhibit the recognition that some people in church are effectively blockers of growth. And removing the blocks on mission often initiates conflict. I suspect that this is the number-one preoccupation of 90 per cent of the parochial clergy I know. They are bogged down in petty struggles with entrenched views. It gradually saps their strength.

The problem is that blockers are often long-standing members of the congregation. They have done a great deal to support the church. Naturally, people don't want to upset them. But, as a church shrinks, it becomes even more reliant on blockers, and the downward spiral continues. It's a cycle that must be broken if a church is to become effective in mission.

One of the hallmarks of a blocker is a proprietorial sense of ownership of all things relating to the church – particularly keys and the fabric of the building. The blocker is the person who asks 'How can I help you?' in a way that sounds much like 'What are you doing here?' The blocker thinks the clergy are here today, gone tomorrow. The blocker sees a problem (often several) in every solution. He or she says things like 'We've tried that before. It didn't work.'

For all the fancy mission initiatives that derive from the diocese downwards, nothing can be more important to the mission of a parish than giving a parish confidence to deal with blockers. The problem is that the Church is deeply distrustful of the type of direct leadership that makes short work of blockages. Instead of the *Henry V* approach ('We are off to invade France – either you are with me or not'), we all have to go in for 'collaborative leadership'.

The fantasy within the whole idea of collaborative leadership is of conflict-free change. As if every situation – blockers included – can be managed by meetings and reports. What suffers in all this political correctness about leadership is the mission of the Church. We need another approach: Once more unto the breach, dear friends, once more.

Are you a Roundhead or a Cavalier?

Church Times, 25 November 2005

Those who think the English Civil War ended in the 17th century ought to take a look at the General Synod. There's definitely a PhD thesis in it for someone. Casting my eye around Synod this year, it struck me that the reasons different factions rub each other up the wrong way might still be best described in terms of Roundheads and Cavaliers.

We can all think of bishops who act like Charles I and have an allergy to synodical government, just as we can immediately recognize all those earnest, soberly dressed lay people up from Huntingdon on an important moral mission.

Roundheads and Cavaliers don't just disagree: they have a deep and visceral dislike of each other's way of being. According to Cavaliers, Roundheads are grim, joyless, prudish, unfunny, provincial, unsophisticated, unsympathetic, cold-hearted, and cruel. According to Roundheads, Cavaliers are self-centred pleasure-seekers, egotistical show-offs, cultural snobs, indifferent to morality, insincere, and obsessed with sex and parties and position.

On top of this basic division, ideology divides yet further. There are left-wing Roundheads (the early Labour Party, Keir Hardie, Rowan Williams), and right-wing Roundheads (Reform, the UK Independence Party, the diocese of Sydney); there are right-wing Cavaliers (parts of Forward in Faith, Alan Clark), and left-wing Cavaliers (champagne socialists, Bill Clinton, me). Forgive the generalizations, but this is only a short column.

The Church of England was expressly set up in order to provide a Church where Roundheads and Cavaliers could coexist without beating each other up. How do we do the same today, and put a stop to the construction of scaffolds?

The Archbishop of Canterbury has called for dialogue between those who disagree. I wonder whether some typology such as the above could serve as a sort of Myers-Briggs for churchmanship. At its best, Myers-Briggs can help squabbling couples recognize that the origins of their mutual bad-temperedness lie in something other than the desire to irritate intentionally.

Another suggestion: perhaps it is best to start a dialogue with those with whom you share at least an ideological or a temperamental affinity. It may be too difficult to start with a double difference. This may be why, for example, I am able to have a delightful lunch with the Principal of Pusey House, as I did last week, but I would think of a visit to the diocese of Sydney as a trip to Mordor. Whatever the difficulties, the motto is simple: it's good to talk.

Chapter 4

Family values

Clergy kids

The *Guardian*, 24 December 2005

Three things I remember about this boy from school, and his name was not one of them. First, he was a rocker: all attitude and acne, all mouth and Motörhead patches. Second, he had the most extensive collection of pornographic magazines in the class. And third, he was the son of a vicar. This third thing wasn't what most interested me about him when I was 13. But it's certainly what interests me now. For having become both a vicar and a father of three, I don't relish the prospect of seeing him or his delinquent sister growing up in the bedrooms down the landing. At the moment, these bedrooms are occupied by little angels. And that's just the worry. For apparently, they're going to be the worst ones of all. Or so goes the familiar story of the vicar's kids.

Why do vicars' children go off the rails? Of course, it's quite possible that they don't any more than anybody else's. It's just that it makes for a great story: straitlaced piety getting its comeuppance through the avenging angel of some foul-mouthed teenager. Yet assuming there is some truth to the stereotype, the idea is that vicars' kids rebel against the claustrophobia of a religious upbringing. Years of Sunday school and altar-serving lead to the inevitable reaction: 'Stuff your religion. I don't want to go to church.' Half Martin Luther, half James Dean, vicars' children tread water at the intersection of the two great rebellious tributaries of modern life: one against the traditions of the Church, the other against one's parents. Authority doesn't stand a chance.

The recently released movie comedy *Keeping Mum* suggests that the reason the Revd Walter Goodfellow's daughter spends her time bouncing around the camper van with any passing goth is that Dad is too otherworldly and socially dysfunctional, too busy trying to perfect his sermon to notice what the kids are up to.

In a sense, the image is part of the problem. For, like clergy themselves, vicars' kids are constantly being defined by other people's weird expectations. Put a bit of white plastic around your neck and most people either patronize you as some bumbling fool, worthy of contempt and pity (just like Rowan Atkinson's the Revd Goodfellow), or they pussyfoot around you with a stumbling reverence – as though sitting uncomfortably in a National Trust tea room. And those trying to wangle a place at the local church school can manage both attitudes at once.

'Hello, is that the Revd Fraser?' goes an awkward voice on the end of the phone five times a day. One day I'll just lose it: 'No, it's not the bloody Revd Fraser. What sort of a rubbish name is that? You wouldn't say: Hello, is that the Right Honourable Blair, would you?' The poor gobsmacked caller wouldn't have a clue what nerve had been tweaked. 'My name is Giles. Or Mr Fraser. Or Dr Fraser if you really must.'

Of course, I'll never have that phone conversation. The caller will have phoned about a funeral. There's always pressure to crawl back inside the box of other people's expectations. It's easier to be what other people want you to be – even if that person is a 19th-century cartoon of a vicar. But my kids don't have to shut up. And they don't.

'I don't like being called good,' says my feisty seven-year-old, Isabella. I don't blame her. It's as if the language of virtue comes as a threat to our identity. Just as novelists find it a challenge to create convincing three-dimensional characters that are also good and virtuous, so the attempt to grow up and discover oneself – a tricky act of discernment at the best of times – can be all but impossible amid the white noise of imputed virtue.

I hate to think how my lot would survive some Christian families. An American Baptist website offering to explain 'How Christian homes produce rock & roll rebels' excoriates liberal parenting and advises children must be raised 'in the nurture and admonition of the Lord' (Ephesians 6.4). Elvis, Jerry Lee Lewis,

Marvin Gaye, Marilyn Manson – they were all brought up in what the website calls 'hypocritical' Christian homes. It argues that the reason Christian kids rebel is because their upbringing isn't Christian enough. The answer is to tighten the Christian screw. 'He that spareth his rod hateth his son' (Proverbs 13.24). Were this policy to be introduced into my Putney vicarage the bang would rattle more windows than a Hemel Hempstead gas leak.

At its worst, Christianity is obsessed with control, transforming the quest for moral virtue into a cage of restrictions. Those spirited kids who fight back deserve admiration. Indeed, they often become the most interesting adults, having learned early on to stand up to those who claim a monopoly on established reality (which is precisely the sort of skill today's Christians need in an overwhelmingly secular society).

Yet those who gag at the craven narcissism of parents who raise their children in order to produce new and improved versions of themselves can be tempted to another extreme: I won't foist my personal moral and religious values on my children. I will wait for them to grow up and then allow them to make these important choices for themselves. It's a familiar line, perhaps the dominant assumption in the moral education of children among the liberal middle classes, and is rooted in a well-intentioned desire to respect the autonomy of one's children.

Yet this reluctance to impose one's values upon one's children is not as straightforward or as honest as it seems. For one thing, there are a great many values that, in reality, most of us would move heaven and earth to have our children share. I don't want my kids to be racist and I have no qualms about, say, gearing their reading so that they are presented with positive images of people with skin a different colour from their own.

This seems uncontroversial. But what about this? Last month my nine-year-old daughter, Alice, joined me at work as I was preparing to greet the Bishop of New Hampshire, the gay bishop that all the foolishness is about in the Anglican Communion. To give Alice a job, I asked her to produce a poster which read 'Welcome to Putney, Bishop Gene'. Of course, the bishop loved it and wrote back a little note. So now Alice is Bishop Gene's greatest fan and is clear that those who don't think he should have been made a bishop are 'silly'. Brainwashing? Or is brainwashing what you call it only when you disagree with the values being promoted?

What's behind the 'think for yourselves' philosophy is the belief that unless we choose our own moral values, those values won't properly be our own. Second-hand morality is like borrowed clothes that won't fit. Only those values that we have made to measure can be counted as authentic and real. It's the instinct behind the view that it's wrong to have a baby christened, or inducted into any belief-system (atheism included), before the age of consent. This is very persuasive and influential stuff. But it's rubbish.

It's rubbish not simply because it's rooted in a consumerist fantasy about choice – as if one could choose morality as one might choose cornflakes. But also for the simple reason that it implies we choose our moral values on impulse and out of nowhere. Refusing the responsibility of providing a moral component to one's child's formation easily leads to inarticulate young adults who have no basis on which to make moral judgements other than on a whim. This is the inarticulacy of the 'wat-ev-err' generation (for full effect listen to Catherine Tate) for whom the word 'good' means nothing more than 'I like it' and 'bad' nothing more than 'I don't like it'. What I really dread to meet on the landing isn't stroppy, moral indignation – it's the indifferent grunt of 'bothered?'

For all these reasons, the Fraser household won't be a value-free environment, and I won't be, indeed I can't be, some kind of neutral umpire in the moral formation of my children. This isn't simply because I'm a vicar – though the moral aspect of how one brings up one's kids is put into focus by my occupation – it's an issue for all parents that is impossible to duck. Nurture abhors a vacuum too.

The anxieties of bringing up kids in the vicarage are not unique. There are other households that are more of a goldfish bowl and where parents are also considered public property. But there can't be many other jobs where, as well as one's own kids, thousands of strangers also want to call you 'Father'. There is a great deal of heartbreak for those families where dad or mum (yes, some female clergy are called 'Mother') take this metaphor so seriously that they spend their life neglecting their own family in the service of their adopted one. Perhaps it's only single clergy that can ever really own the title 'Father'. I remain haunted by a comment made to a colleague of mine by his grown-up son: 'You have sacrificed our family on the altar of your principles.'

In search of a play ethic

Church Times, 27 August 2004

Exactly 100 years ago, the sociologist Max Weber published *The Protestant Ethic and the Spirit of Capitalism*. In a now famous argument, Weber sought to expose the theological roots of the Protestant work ethic.

'Why should I let the toad *work* / Squat on my life?' asked Philip Larkin. Weber said that you could blame the crowded commuter train and long enslaved hours on the Calvinist belief in predestination.

Some of us are saved and some not. All is predetermined, and there is nothing we can do to change our fate. The question then becomes: which category am I in – am I saved or not? Into this increasingly anxious self-absorption about one's salvation comes a strange thought process. Salvation issues in godly living. So those who lead godly lives are likely to be the ones who have been saved. So I must lead a godly life: get up early, polish my shoes, work hard, pray a great deal, be financially successful, and so on.

There are more holes in the logic than in a Swiss cheese. Furthermore, the great irony is that a belief system designed to eliminate the Pelagian connection between work and salvation serves only to reinforce it. Beware of Christians in suits.

By contrast, let me suggest a different theological paradigm. As the summer holidays draw to a close, and the trips to the zoo and the beach have dried up, late August again delivers the highlight of the season: the show. As boredom ignites creativity, the children transform the garden into a proscenium arch of swings, buckets, and washing lines. Isabella sits for hours, making tickets. A play is endlessly rehearsed and the casting bitterly contested. Adults are then dragooned into place for a half-hour of princesses and chaos. It is wonderful, bizarre, and entirely pointless.

Here is a much healthier theological paradigm than the anxious instrumentality of the Protestant work ethic. Perhaps it's naff to call it the Catholic play ethic: still, here is a joyous celebration of life which is not designed to elicit any advantage. It's godly play: an act of thanksgiving for freedom, gardens and friendship. These things are celebrated in and of themselves, not because they advance any cause. Like the Eucharist, the show is holiday as thanksgiving.

One of the ancient rabbis tells the story that the first question God will ask when you meet is this: 'Many blessings I have sent your way: have you availed yourself of them?' Well, have you?

Suffer little children

The *Guardian*, 8 June 2006

Pretty much all I remember from my prep school are the beatings: that lonely wait outside the headmaster's study; the cane, the slipper, the table tennis bat. I remember my underpants filled with blood. I remember seething with frustration when they beat my brother. My mother had asked me to look after him. But there was nothing I could do as he was led towards the study in his little tartan dressing gown.

That was 30 years ago, but in time measured out by the psyche it was yesterday. Thank God such things are now illegal.

But there remain those determined to turn back the clock. 'We are told that in England it is a crime to spank children,' writes Debbi Pearl from No Greater Joy Ministries, following a row that has erupted over the distribution of their literature in the UK. 'Therefore Christians are not able to openly obey God in regard to biblical chastisement. They are in danger of having the state steal their children.'

The Pearls are evangelical Christians who believe corporal punishment is 'doing it God's way'. With a mailing list of tens of thousands of parents, the Pearls say that the justification for their approach is in scripture: 'He that spareth his rod hateth his son: but he that loveth him chasteneth him betimes' (Proverbs 13.24).

Chastening begins early. 'For the under-one-year-old, a little, 10- to 12-inch long, willowy branch (stripped of any knots that might break the skin) about one-eighth inch diameter is sufficient,' writes Michael Pearl. With older children he advises: 'After a short explanation about bad attitudes and the need to love, patiently and calmly apply the rod to his backside. Somehow, after eight or 10 licks, the poison is transformed into gushing love and contentment. The world becomes a beautiful place. A brand-new child emerges. It makes an adult stare at the rod in wonder, trying to see what magic is contained therein.'

It's incredible to me that books such as this are readily available on Amazon; it is little short of incitement to child abuse. What makes the whole thing doubly sick is that it's done in the name of God. Apparently, the 'proper application of the rod is essential to the Christian worldview'. Note 'essential'. Perhaps it shouldn't come as a surprise. For, as evangelicals, the Pearls believe that salvation only comes through punishment and pain. God punishes his Son with crucifixion so that humanity might not have to face the Father's anger. This image of God the Father, for whom violence is an expression of tough love, is lodged deep in the evangelical imagination. And it twists a religion of forgiveness and compassion into something dark and cruel.

It's terrifying how deep this teaching penetrates into a philosophy of child-rearing. Just as divine anger is deemed to be

provoked by the original sin of human disobedience, the beating of children is seen as punishment for rebellion. According to
Ted Tripp, in his monstrous bestseller *Shepherding a Child's
Heart*, even babies who struggle while having their nappy
changed are deemed to be rebellious and need punishment.

Last month Lynn Paddock of North Carolina was charged
with the murder of her four-year-old son, Sean. She had apparently beaten him with a length of quarter-inch plumbing line –
plastic tubing. Like many in her church, Paddock had turned to
the Pearls' resources on biblical parenting. The Pearls say
chastisement with plumbing line is 'a real attention getter'. Sean
Paddock's autopsy describes layers of bruises stretching from
his bottom to his shoulder.

What Jesus said about those who would harm children comes
inevitably to mind: 'It would be better for them if a millstone
was hanged about their neck, and that they were drowned in the
depth of the sea.'

The evangelicals who like to giftwrap
Islamophobia

The *Guardian*, 10 November 2003

It all sounds innocent enough. Operation Christmas Child 'is a
unique ministry that brings Christmas joy, packed in gift-filled
shoeboxes, to children around the world'. Over the past 10
years, 24 million shoeboxes have been delivered, making it the
world's largest children's Christmas project. Every US president
since Ronald Reagan has packed a shoebox for Operation
Christmas Child. In the UK, thousands of schools, churches and
youth clubs are doing the same. Some will fill their boxes with
dried-out felt-tip pens and discarded Barbie amputees. Others
spend serious money on the latest Game Boy or Sony Walkman.

But what many parents and teachers don't know is that

behind Operation Christmas Child is the evangelical charity Samaritan's Purse. Their aim is 'the advancement of the Christian faith through educational projects and the relief of poverty'. And a particularly toxic version of Christianity it is. This is the same outfit that targeted Eastern Europe after the fall of the Berlin Wall and was widely condemned for following US troops into Iraq to claim Muslims for Christ.

It's run by the Revd Franklin Graham – chosen by George Bush to deliver the prayers at his presidential inauguration – who has called Islam 'a very wicked and evil religion'. Graham, the son of the evangelist Billy Graham, is from the same school of thought as General William Boykin, US deputy under-secretary of defence for intelligence, who described America as waging a holy war against 'the idol' of Islam's false god and 'a guy called Satan' who 'wants to destroy us as a Christian army'.

Across the UK, children in multicultural schools are being encouraged to support a scheme that is, quite understandably, deeply offensive to Muslims. Under pressure from those who have complained that Operation Christmas Child is a way of promoting Christian fundamentalism through toys, evangelical literature will now be distributed alongside shoebox parcels from the UK rather than inside them – as if this makes any real difference. Little wonder that such organizations as the fire service in South Wales, which had allowed its depots to be used as collection points for shoeboxes, has decided to suspend its involvement. Other organizations are reconsidering their participation.

What is most resented about Samaritan's Purse is the way it links aid and evangelism. 'We have no problem with people going into a country to do evangelical work,' said Hodan Hassan, a spokeswoman for the Council on American-Islamic Relations. 'But when you mix humanitarian work in a war-torn country with evangelization you create a problem. You have desperate people and you have someone who has food in one hand and a Bible in another.'

Christian missionaries in 19th-century India used to describe those who came to the mission stations simply for food as 'rice Christians'. This became a derogatory term for those driven to accept Christianity out of hunger rather than genuine conviction. The accusation is that groups such as Samaritan's Purse are creating a new generation of rice Christians in the Middle East. How might they be stopped? The answer is not quite as simple as erecting a firewall between Christian evangelism and social action. For Christianity is not neatly divisible into theory and practice; it is a form of praxis. Belief and action are ultimately inseparable.

Ironically, it is the story of the Good Samaritan that provides one of the most effective put-downs to precisely the sort of Islamophobia displayed by Christian fundamentalists such as Graham. Jesus is asked: 'Who is my neighbour?' The moral of the story he tells in response – at least the one most people remember from Sunday school – is that it is the man who is beaten up and left for dead that Jesus points to as our neighbour. Conclusion: we must help those in need.

But that's not the story at all. A man is mugged in the Wadi Qelt between Jerusalem and Jericho. Whereas the religious pass by and do nothing, it is the Samaritan who offers care. Those listening to the story would have despised Samaritans. The words 'good' and 'Samaritan' just didn't go together. Indeed, theirs would have been the General Boykin reaction: that Samaritans worshipped the idol of a false god. Therefore, in casting the Samaritan as the only passer-by with compassion, Jesus is making an all-out assault on the prejudices of his listeners.

If the story was just about helping the needy, whoever they are, it would have been sufficient to cast the Samaritan as the victim and a Jewish layperson as the person who helped. Crucially, however, the hated Samaritan is held up as the moral exemplar. Conclusion: we must overcome religious bigotry.

The story of the Good Samaritan, in the hands of Franklin Graham, is conscripted as propaganda for the superiority of Christian compassion to the brutal indifference of other religions – almost the opposite of the purpose of the story.

What is astonishing is that Christian fundamentalists have managed to persuade millions that their warped version of Christianity is the real thing and that mainstream churches have sold out to the secular spirit of the age. The truth is quite the reverse.

US evangelicals employ a selective biblical literalism to support a theology that systematically confuses the kingdom of God with the US's burgeoning empire. It is no coincidence that the mission fields most favoured by US evangelicals are also the targets of neo-conservative military ambition. To use Jesus as the rallying cry for a new imperialism is the most shameful reversal of all, for he was murdered by the forces of empire. The cross spoke of Roman power in just the way Black Hawk helicopters speak today of US power.

Schools and churches that are getting their children involved in Operation Christmas Child need to be aware of the agenda their participation is helping to promote. There is, of course, a huge emotional hit in wrapping up a shoebox for a Christmas child. But if we are to teach our children properly about giving, we must wean them off the feel-good factor.

Instead, why not support Christian Aid, which works wherever the need and regardless of religion. Its current campaigns include working with HIV/AIDS orphans in Kenya, recycling guns in Mozambique, and highlighting the impact of world trade rules on farmers in Ghana. Sure, we will need to have some rather grown-up conversations with our children if we are to explain some of these things. But that would be time better spent than wrapping up a shoebox. We must get over our fondness for charity and develop a thirst for justice.

The scary world of pre-teens

Church Times, 30 April 2004

In the midst of bath-time chaos, my eight-year-old daughter Alice drops a bombshell: 'Daddy, what's snogging?' Sensing my fear, she wiggles her tongue in the air. Her younger sister looks on, amused, not quite understanding, but appreciating that

Daddy is on the ropes. A diversionary manoeuvre saves the day, but the questions are coming thick and fast, and I'm not sure I am prepared.

Earlier on, a dozen of Alice's friends came for her birthday party. Most of them brought Bratz girls, the new dolls that are taking market-share away from the 44-year-old Barbie. In the first part of this year, Barbie sales slumped, while sales of Bratz girls have risen by 77 per cent. Unlike the demure blonde who inhabits a fairy-tale world of horse-riding and castles, and who seems forever on the lookout for a handsome prince, Bratz girls have sassy urban attitude. Ethnically diverse, they wear cropped tops and trainers.

They are not interested in finding husbands; they hang out with their girlfriends in coffee shops discussing lippy and CDs – and sniggering about snogging. Just as the 1950s saw the invention of the teenager, now the pre-teen is emerging as a distinct cultural identity. The high street now offers a type of coffee for this age-range: the babyccino.

Part of me prefers the world of the Bratz to that of Barbie. Bratz can look after themselves, and they are not going to be fooled by the first Ken who rides into the magical kingdom of their childhood. Whereas Barbie has been blamed for the idealization of an anorexic body shape, Jasmin, Jade, Chloe and their friends are caricatures of trendy teenagers, with oversized heads and feet, who nevertheless pose a new set of worries for the anxious parent. Bratz lips look as if they have had collagen implants, and thus a pout too obviously prepared for snogging.

Even so, the games my girls play with their dolls are fun and imaginative. Instead of acting out a Barbie fantasy of middle-class domesticity with a sequin make-over, the Bratz girls find their entertainment in friendship and chit-chat. It might seem trivial, but these role-plays teach children about social interaction in ways Barbie did not.

Yet Bratz remain self-absorbed. The first question in any social situation seems to concern what to wear. I want my children to be capable, confident and caring. The Bratz generation is certainly confident, and possibly capable. But is it caring?

Quavers or Wotsits: the big debate

Church Times, 18 August 2006

The child psychologist Dr Tanya Byron is one of those celebrity experts who has made a whole bunch of TV programmes dealing with difficult kids. I have seen a few of them, but I can't quite take her seriously. To me, she will always be the wicked witch. I am always the prince, my brother the fearsome dragon and her sister the beautiful princess.

No, you don't need to reach for your Freud. Every year throughout my childhood, Tanya's family and my family would go on holiday to Frinton, where the kids would always make up a play for the adults. Summer after summer, we enjoyed hours of haggling of casting, costume design and rehearsals – and then the chaos of performance, utterly incoherent to the audience of delighted adults. They were some of the magic moments of my childhood.

Now, more than 30 years later, I am in Frinton with my kids, enjoying sun, sand and Scrabble. We spend hours making up games and talking wondrous rubbish. I have just spent half an hour helping to compile a league table of crisps, and refereeing a hot debate on the respective merits of Quavers and Wotsits.

Recently, there has been a running debate in the letters pages of this paper on the question of whether a priest is, first of all, called to be or to do. I tend instinctively to side with the doers. After all, isn't 'being' just a theology of lolling around, achieving nothing and then giving it a spurious justification. What rubbish is that – we have pews to fill. Given views like this, it is little wonder that I have a reputation among my family for not liking holidays.

Yet, halfway through this one I remember why they are so important. Like many clerics, I am way too task-orientated. At worst, this means that I try and convert everything (and I guess that often includes people) into tools, in the pursuit of certain ends. It's quite a confession: sometimes, even my most precious relationships are driven by instrumentality.

But it is only now, arguing pointless rubbish with my kids, that I spot it. Holidays are not best understood as recharging one's batteries so as to make us more effective at work – the instrumentalist view of them. Surely it is better to think of them as reminding us of a world beyond all talk of effectiveness and league tables. A disputation of crisps returns me to a world of joy unencumbered by success. Perhaps that's why Jesus says that unless you see the world like little children, you won't enter the kingdom of heaven.

My gran's dementia

Church Times, 17 June 2005

As the elderly lady leaves church, she thanks me for the service. I respond by giving her a big squeeze and a kiss. As she totters off, I hear her complaining about the over-familiarity of the vicar. I chuckle: she is my gran, who has had dementia for years, and no longer knows who I am.

Back in her care home, she has persuaded fellow residents that she was once a nun from St Joseph's. To complement this new identity, Sister Audrey (as she calls herself) has found a remarkable silver Lurex wraparound top.

My family has been getting nuttier. The other week, my mum, who is president of the local Women's Institute, started a Peter Kay 'Show me the way to Amarillo' conga in the lighting department of John Lewis in Peterborough. For her, respectability and free-spiritedness battle it out, and a certain middle-English eccentricity usually wins. But for my gran it's different. Dementia has brought about an Indian summer of happiness in what has been a tough and often unhappy life.

Those who suffer from senile dementia often lose their worries about what other people think of them. For some, this can mean an unkempt appearance and a broader command of Anglo-Saxon than the blushing relatives ever remembered. But those who, like my gran, have fought against a debilitating sense of social inferiority all their lives, are released from this dreadful burden. We hear a great deal about old people's homes being God's waiting-rooms, reeking of neglect and incontinence. But, for Sister Audrey, it may well be the place where she has finally come into her own.

'Re-clothe us in our rightful mind,' we sing. Yes, but what is our rightful mind? I met Iris Murdoch a couple of times – once after she had just given a lecture on Plato, and years later, when she was lost and confused in the University Church in Oxford. Surely, it was the mind of the erudite don that was Iris Murdoch's 'rightful mind'. Yet, for my gran, most of her life was characterized by a crushing nervousness and anxiety. Only now, as she looks after her fellow residents, and starts to experiment with her wardrobe, does she give some indication of the person she might have been, had she been liberated from her demons.

I wonder; could it be, for some of us, that it's only when our schemes have all gone foggy that we are released to become the people God really wants us to be?

Chapter 5

The war on fundamentalism

Fundamentally speaking

The *Guardian*, 23 July 2005

Muslims who preach hate are to be deported and subject to new restrictions, Charles Clarke announced in the Commons on Wednesday. So what would the home secretary have to say about stuff like this: 'Blessed is he who takes your little children and smashes their heads against the rocks'? Or this: 'O God, break the teeth in their mouths . . . Let them be like the snail that dissolves into slime; like the untimely birth that never sees the sun . . . The righteous will bathe their feet in the blood of the wicked.' No, this is not Islam, it is the Bible. And there is a lot more where that came from.

Why, then, are so many commentators persuaded that the Qur'an is a manual of hate – compared to the Judeo-Christian Scriptures, it is very tame stuff indeed. More disturbing still for Christians and Jews, the nearest scriptural justification for suicide bombings I can think of comes from the book of Judges, where Samson pushes apart the structural supports of a temple packed with people. 'Let me die with the Philistines,' he prays, just before the building collapses.

It will not do to work with a Bible of the nice bits or allegorize these passages out of existence, leaving them hanging around for future fanatics to exploit. Religion must openly acknowledge its own dirty secrets.

All of the above may simply encourage those who think that religion itself is the problem. After all, it is precisely the non-negotiability of the divine commandment that makes peaceful religious politics so elusive. If the choice is between the ballot box and divine will, how can the faithful remain committed to democratic decision-making?

The campaigning secularist has no shortage of ammunition.

Many of their criticisms are well aimed and need to be taken extremely seriously. As the great Islamic philosopher Averroes put it: 'Truth never fears honest debate.' But the problem with the secular attack is that it refuses to make any sort of distinction between good religion and bad religion.

The assumption is that bad religion – the sex-obsessed religion of violence and superstition – is the real thing, and that good religion – the religion that encourages peace and respect for human life – is a modern fake, a religion that disingenuously reinvents itself to reflect modern values and consequently does not entirely believe what it says.

The truth, however, is that rigid fundamentalism is the modern fake. Most belief systems have huge and historic recourses of self-criticism. The Gospels contain some of the most biting attacks on pathological religiosity; the Hebrew prophets are involved in a constant campaign of subversion against the misplaced theology of narrow sectarianism. As Isaiah has it: 'When you stretch out your hands, I will hide my eyes from you; even though you make many prayers, I will not listen, your hands are full of blood.'

These theological recourses are precious and need to be nurtured. But a wholesale cultural assault upon a religious tradition does nothing to help more moderate voices. A religion that sees itself as being under attack is less sympathetic to those who would argue from within. In such circumstances, self-criticism is easily represented as disloyalty. Yet now, more than ever, we need to encourage those able to use theology to speak out against violence done in God's name.

Like many, I do not know Islam well enough. I am sure that, for many millions, it is a religion of peace; I am sure there is currently a theological struggle for its very soul. What I have yet to understand – because it has not been sufficiently well explained to me, or given sufficient exposure in the media – is how murderous jihad is a theological heresy.

These are the voices that we desperately need to hear. The help that can be offered by Christians and others is our own admission that the complicity of religion with acts of violence is something Islam does not face alone.

Beware the Bible traffic wardens

Church Times, 11 November 2005

I have never warmed to church documents – like the communiqué recently issued by the Churches of the Global South – that pepper every paragraph with bracketed chapter and verse references to the Bible. It's not because I want to distance theological disputation from the Bible. Quite the reverse, it's because this way of referencing the text can profoundly distort what the Bible is trying to say.

It is worth remembering that early Bibles had no chapter and verse referencing whatsoever. Eusebius of Caesarea began to categorize each Gospel into numbered sections, but the first New Testament to have anything like our modern divisions of chapters and verses was published by the printer Robert Estienne in 1550. These divisions did not fall from heaven: he made them up on the long journeys between his two presses in Paris and Lyon. Over the broad sweep of Christian history, chapter and verse theology is a distinctly modern invention.

Of course, it's a convenience and helps the reader find her way about. But what it has also done is give the impression that biblical truth exists at the level of individual sentences – as if the Bible is built up, truth by truth, as one might build a house out of bricks. The only other thing we read like that is letters we get from the solicitor or instructions on how to assemble an IKEA wardrobe. For the most part, when we read a piece of literature, we allow it to disclose its message over many pages. The meaning is revealed within the narrative as a whole.

Imagine how different it would be if we had to find our way around the Bible by referring to passages as 'You know, that bit that comes after He turned water into wine'. After all, that is how the stories were known for many years. And reading the text without those distracting numbers allows the narrative to flow and the imagination to spark. Suddenly, one is dealing with a wonderful and extraordinary collection of poetries, parables and histories rather than a 1,000-piece jigsaw puzzle.

I'm afraid I can't help but think of those who constantly refer to chapter and verse as the traffic wardens of the biblical scene. It's the sort of theology employed by those who use the Bible to control people rather than inspire them.

Eating the scroll

Church Times, 7 November 2003

Unlikely as it may sound, my theology book of the year is about cooking: Julian Barnes's *The Pedant in the Kitchen* (Atlantic Books, 2003). Barnes suggests that there are two sorts of cooks: those who slavishly follow a recipe, and those who are more instinctive, who cook by faith and not by sight.

I'm more the latter. The kitchen looks like a bomb blast in a delicatessen after a few hours of my culinary creativity. Though I affect the pose of a cook who simply needs to tap into the muse, like everyone else, I look things up in Delia when no one else is watching.

Cooks like me are terribly snooty about the need for a recipe book – 'as if cooking from a text were like making love with a sex manual open at your elbow', as Barnes memorably puts it. We prefer the casual confidence of Jamie Oliver to the buttoned-up formality of Mrs Beaton.

Julian Barnes, however, is a self-confessed pedant. What is a medium-sized onion, he worries? How big is a lump, or how many strawberries are there in a handful? Latitude is the pedant's torment. But, while laughing at his own expense, Barnes lands some well-aimed blows at the casual cook. 'Oh, that'll do' is not a phrase often heard in top restaurant kitchens. For the most part, he insists, originality is actually theft. Furthermore, even the best cooks have the recipe on hand to guide them.

At a number of points, Barnes subtly encourages the idea that this is also a comment about using the Bible. Scales fell from my eyes as he represented pedantry in a positive light as patient attention to the text and as taking care. Could this be a way into a more sympathetic understanding of biblical literalism? Furthermore, could the fear of literalism be turning people like me towards the casual hermeneutics of 'Oh, that'll do'?

Barnes's explanation for his own form of culinary autism is that he began to cook later in life. The kitchen, like the marital bed, the voting booth and the pew, were places he was protected from during his childhood. The late convert often makes up for a lack of confidence by sticking rigidly to the text.

Forgetting that recipes begin as oral tradition, the pedant in the kitchen finds the uncharted waters of imaginative extension unsettling. More problematically, by being obsessed by the size of the onions, the pedant can often miss the whole purpose of great cooking: to share and to nurture. At its best, cooking is neither art nor science, but an imaginative act of love taking care. Not a bad hermeneutic for reading the Bible.

Book club bullies

The *Guardian*, 28 June 2004

Fur has been flying in the small Gloucestershire village of Brimscombe. Local boy done good Nick Page, who hosts the BBC2 programme *Escape to the Country*, was to be the star guest at the local fête. But just half an hour before the start he pulled out, objecting to Christian propaganda displayed on one of the stalls. 'We've got a Christian fundamentalist prime minister sending hundreds of people to their death every week and I couldn't believe people were promoting these ideas – at a village fête of all places,' he said.

Page is right to highlight the fact that Christian fundamentalism is creeping into the heart of middle England. But to describe the prime minister as a fundamentalist is flippant nonsense that seriously misplaces the meaning of the term. Using the F-word as a generalized insult for all those with religious convictions allows the real thing to slip by unchallenged.

Fundamentalism was first employed in southern California in the 1920s and rapidly gained an audience among Southern Baptists keen to reclaim what they perceived as Christian fundamentals against the onslaught of secular modernity and liberal theology. It's now a portmanteau concept applied to many religious fringe groups in all the world's faiths, and spans huge differences in theological temperament.

The common denominator is a refusal to accept that a sacred text can be legitimately read in more than one way. This goes hand in hand with the belief that Scripture has a straightforward meaning, often twisted by clever sophistry dancing to secular tunes of gay liberation, feminism, socialism, and so on. Fundamentalism is not about the degree of religious conviction or about having beliefs that are non-negotiable – all but the most cynically pragmatic of us have those. Terry Eagleton gets it right: 'It is a textual affair.'

Yet it is precisely here that fundamentalism is most vulnerable, for the written word is wholly unsuited to the transmission of a single message. A text, particularly one as fecund and multilayered as the Bible, cannot be ring-fenced. Meaning scatters off the page in a multiplicity of directions. Ironically, for the fundamentalist, the text turns out to be the very source of the problem.

It is no coincidence that fundamentalism flourishes in places of low literacy. The US Bible belt is not a place where books are commonly read for pleasure or enlightenment: information comes from the radio and TV. For all their emphasis on the sacred text, fundamentalists are generally unfamiliar with the culture of books.

Salman Rushdie captured this fundamentalist suspicion of the text perfectly in *Haroun and the Sea of Stories*, in which the fundamentalist character Khattam-Shud seeks to close of the diversity of interpretations by blocking the source of the Streams of Story. 'He looked into the water and saw that it was made up of a thousand thousand thousand and one different currents, each one a different colour, weaving in and out of one another like a liquid tapestry of breathtaking complexity; and because the stories were held in fluid form, they retained the ability to change, to become new versions of themselves, to join up with other stories and so become yet other stories.' This is precisely the sort of hermeneutic chaos the fundamentalist finds so insufferable and against which he can never win. Like Khattam-Shud, the fundamentalist prefers a text to be lifeless.

Of course, the reasons for resisting the idea that a text requires interpretation are social and political, not principally theological. Fundamentalism flourishes in places of instability and social vulnerability. It is the desire for solid foundations in a world in which the vulnerable are tossed about like flies to wanton boys.

Often this is associated with poverty, but not always. Students I see arriving at Oxford for the first time are pitched into a new and uncertain world. In such circumstances students commonly find refuge in a church that gives them the security of a singular message believed with absolute and unquestioning certainty. For those at the rough end of global capitalism or American imperialism, the instinct is considerably more urgent.

Once a month my wife goes to her book club. Everyone is given space to express what they made of the latest choice of novel. Others listen courteously: sometimes enlightened, sometimes puzzled. No one interpretation claims dominance.

The fundamentalist is the bully of the religious book club determined to regulate the conversation and silence disagreement. Even within the traditionally inclusive Church of England these book club bullies are increasingly using political muscle to change the rules of the conversation so that only those who subscribe to a particular interpretation of the text can participate. Elsewhere, this muscle is exercised at the point of a gun.

Perhaps I am insufferably liberal, but we need to have a greater appreciation of why bullies become bullies. Fundamentalism can only be defeated if we understand it.

Evangelicals against racism

The *Guardian*, 3 May 2006

Over the past few months there has been growing evidence of a developing alliance between the British National Party and fundamentalist evangelicals. Superficially, a marriage made in heaven (or should that be hell?) – both are right-wing extremists with a love of publicity and a hatred for progressive Britain. What's interesting is that their passionate liaison has ended in tears. It's a failed love affair that will encourage those who fear the emergence in this country of the alliances between right-wing Christians and right-wing secularists that are commonly forged on the other side of the Atlantic.

It all started amicably enough. 'We are a secular political party,' said BNP spokesman Phil Edwards. 'But people are worried at the political correctness of the Church of England and the Islamification of Britain.' In response to these twin evils, BNP members helped to set up the 'Christian Council of Britain'.

'The BNP were approached by a group of disaffected ladies and gentlemen who felt their traditional Christian views were not being represented by the liberal-left spokesmen in the Anglican Church,' they explained. Following this conversion experience, the BNP even found someone with reverend before his name to theologize party policy. 'The mixing of races challenges the glory of God,' said the Revd Bob West.

Last month, a media-watch organization started spotting the same faces that appear at BNP rallies regularly appearing at protests over *Jerry Springer – the Opera*. Local BNP leader Graham Green said: 'We are totally opposed to this theatre production, and our members have been helping to hand out pro-Christian leaflets.' But the BNP hadn't quite thought through their new association. For fundamentalist Christians from organizations like Christian Voice are committed to the literal truth of Genesis: that all human beings are descended from Adam and Eve. Because of this, the human race is of 'one blood' (Acts 17.26).

Despite all their talk of supporting 'traditional Christians' – an increasingly transparent euphemism for fundamentalists – the idea that all human beings share a common parentage was a tradition too far for the BNP. Racists have always found it easier to warp the theory of evolution, arguing, as Edwards recently did, 'that white people are more highly evolved than blacks'. Within weeks of setting up the Christian Council of Britain, the alliance was in tatters. 'If you don't believe in Darwinian evolution then you are even dafter than you appear,' the BNP told the national director of Christian Voice, Stephen Green. The love affair was over.

For the BNP, Christian is just another word for white, just as Islamic has become another word for Asian. Now that the religious hatred bill has been watered down, groups like the BNP are free to use religious affiliation as code for race, translating illegal incitement to racial hatred into legal incitement to religious hatred. Here, then, is the incentive for the BNP to establish a church group or cosy up to Christian fundamentalists.

But what is so utterly ridiculous about the BNP's desire to defend 'Christian culture' is that the vast majority of Christians in the world are not white. The average Anglican, for instance, is a black woman living in Africa. Moreover, if Jesus were ever to walk this green and pleasant land, the BNP would be committed to his repatriation. Even their great love of St George is a joke: George was either Turkish or Palestinian, and his legend migrated to this country from the Middle East.

What is fascinating about the ill-fated combination of the BNP and Christian Voice is that it demonstrates how deeply resistant Christianity is to all forms of racism. It has not always been apparent that this was the case. After all, Christianity had a hand in slavery and apartheid. But Christianity also played a decisive role in the dismantling of both. For every bigot wanting to exploit Christianity in the service of racist ideology, there is a Wilberforce or a Tutu reminding Christians of what's in the Bible.

'In Christ there is neither Jew nor Greek, for you are all one in Christ Jesus,' says St Paul. Racial categories and nationality are deemed of no importance for those whose identity is primarily found in Christ. It's an expression of a basic truth of monotheism: God is the God of all. In church, we are all brothers and sisters. This is why churches are some of the most important points of racial integration in our society.

Some years ago I was a priest on a tough council estate in Walsall. It was classic recruiting territory for National Front thugs. And it was undoubtedly these same thugs that put bricks through the stained-glass windows after the church invited a black gospel choir to come and sing. Rarely have I been as proud of churchgoers as I was of those wonderful old dears who would shuffle along to mass, clutching their Bibles, in open defiance of the skinheads.

In recent weeks the Methodist Church has set up a useful website called Countering Political Extremism in which the views of the major churches have been compiled. It's one of the few theological points upon which all churches agree: you cannot be a Christian and a racist. The United Reformed Church is the most specific: 'Any form of support for organizations such as the BNP is incompatible with Christian discipleship.'

Don't hand religion to the right

(written together with Dr William Whyte)

The *Guardian*, 18 March 2005

For decades, the political class on this side of the Atlantic has prided itself on the absence of religious culture wars. The obsession with abortion, gay marriage and obscenity, the alliance between the secular and religious right – these are peculiarly American pathologies. It couldn't happen here. After all, we're just not religious enough.

Except it does seem to be happening here. In making abortion an election issue, Michael Howard has prompted the Archbishop of Westminster, Cardinal Cormac Murphy-O'Connor, pointedly to warn against assuming 'that Catholics would be more in support of the Labour Party'. Elsewhere, the Christian right targets the BBC, and the Church of England is being colonized by homophobic evangelicals with broad smiles and loads of PR savvy. No wonder the cogs are whirring at Conservative central office on how best to exploit the voting power of religion.

In contrast, the left continues to push religion away. They 'don't do God', in Alastair Campbell's famous phrase. Even those politicians of the left who 'do God' privately have to be effectively outed, as Ruth Kelly was over her membership of Opus Dei. It never used to be like this. There has long been an affinity between the Church and the left. The Liberal Party was sustained by the so-called nonconformist conscience and the Labour Party famously derived more from Methodism than Marx – Keir Hardie once describing socialism as 'the embodiment of Christianity in our industrial system'. Later both CND and the anti-apartheid movement were inspired by Christian socialism.

Even comparatively recently things were looking up for the religious left. Tony Blair is a member of the Christian socialist movement and in Rowan Williams the Church of England has a self-confessed 'bearded lefty' at the top. Yet instead of a renaissance there has been a decline. The Archbishop of Canterbury is now a virtual prisoner of the religious right. And Labour Christians seem silent and impotent. How did we get to here?

In the first place, the religious left has found itself constantly challenged by the secular left. While the religious right and neo-conservatives have worked together, progressives have split and split again. Blair is too embarrassed to talk the language of faith because he knows it would alienate his allies. Some object to religion on principle. Others insist that a Christian response is inevitably intolerant, exclusive, even racist. So left secularists welcomed Jubilee 2000 but ignored the fact that the jubilee is a biblical concept.

But progressive Christians also seem incapable of confronting the religious right on its own terms. Jesus offered a political manifesto that emphasized non-violence, social justice and the redistribution of wealth – yet all this is drowned out by those who use the text to justify a narrow, authoritarian and morally judgemental form of social respectability. The irony is that the religious right and the secular left have effectively joined forces to promote the idea that the Bible is reactionary. For the secular left, the more the Bible can be described in this way, the easier it is to rubbish. Thus the religious right is free to claim a monopoly on Christianity. And the Christian left, hounded from both sides, finds itself shouted into silence.

Does this matter? Well, yes. Religion isn't going away; if anything, it is making a comeback. Nearly three-quarters of the population declared themselves Christian in the 2001 census. The old belief that religion would wither and die has been exposed as simplistic. In this environment, the secular left needs to suspend worn-out hostilities and realize that many people of faith are fellow travellers in the fight for social justice. Otherwise, the coalition of Christian and secular conservatives will grow stronger. That will further damage the Church, turning it into an intolerant sect. But it will also undermine progressive politics.

All of which requires a new courage from the Christian left. They need to toughen up, get organized and invoke the spirit of millions of Christians, from St Francis to Donald Soper, who have fought against injustice throughout the ages. Twenty years ago, Faith in the City was a prophetic call to Britain, condemning the selfishness of Thatcherism and the greed of 1980s Britain. The current campaign, Make Poverty History, is a similarly significant moment.

But the present situation also demands a reassessment by the secular left of the religious left. Because only the religious left is capable of challenging the religious right with the language of faith. The secular left, in short, needs to stop sniping and start making new friends. In America, the Christian right and the neocons have grown strong by working together. Now so must we.

Blessed are the jokers

The *Guardian*, 27 September 2004

'He went up there from Bethel; and while he was going up on the way, some small boys came out of the city and jeered at him saying, "Go away, baldy! Go away, baldy!" When he turned around and saw them, he cursed them in the name of the Lord. Then two she-bears came out of the woods and mauled 42 of the boys' (2 Kings 2.23–24).

Apparently, the prophet Elisha couldn't take a joke. And neither, it seems, can the 6,000 Christians who have successfully petitioned the director general of the BBC to scrap plans to show the Vatican cartoon comedy *Popetown*. Apparently, depicting the Pope on a pogo stick (with voice by Ruby Wax) surrounded by scheming cardinals is likely to offend believers and threaten their faith. Well, I'm offended too. But unlike the 6,000, I'm offended by the implication that, as a Christian, I am a humourless oversensitive wimp whose faith requires special protection. I'm offended by always being classed alongside the offended.

For being offended by the prospect of the Pope on a pogo stick is a transparent form of passive/aggressive manipulation – casting oneself as the hard-done-to victim while pulling all the strings. Using the mock innocent vulnerability of 'being offended' as a weapon with which to make others do things your way is never going to win any friends.

Moreover, it is precisely because religious people get in a huff so very easily that they are so funny. The reason you can't stop sniggering in church is because of the perceived disapproval of others. Without the disapproval, there's nothing to laugh about. Ironically, therefore, it's the 6,000 outraged Christians and all the others like them that keep the writers of *Popetown*, *Father Ted* and *The Life of Brian* in business. The best way to become an object of fun is to act like the boot-faced Puritan relatives that went to stay with Edmund Blackadder.

At what point, I wonder, did Christians lose their sense of humour? Dairmaid MacCulloch begins his great work on the

Reformation in the small English country church at Preston Blisset in Buckinghamshire. Looking up from behind the altar the priest cannot avoid noticing the carving of an ample early-14th-century arse directed straight towards him. Professor MacCulloch doesn't know its purpose but reminds us that 'this was a religion where shouts of laughter as well as roars of rage were common in church, where the clergy waged a constant if perhaps sometimes half-hearted battle against the invasion of fun'.

Ridiculing the Church, the clergy, bishops and the Pope has a long history. For early Protestants, the ecclesiastical establishment represented by the Pope was perceived as an instrument of domination and self-serving power. In Umberto Eco's *The Name of the Rose*, the monastery librarian finds Aristotle's lost work in praise of comedy. Realizing its potential to undermine the status quo, he poisons its pages. The moral of which is that the Church is afraid of laughter because laughter is impossible to control.

It is little wonder that the earthier reformers used laughter as a weapon against the Vatican. Unlike many of today's Christians, the Luther who offered the Pope 'a fart for a staff' cared little about giving offence. Not that causing offensive was the end purpose. For Luther, humour was a way to cast down the mighty from their thrones. Humour works to expose the pious, the pompous and the arrogant. Laughter is the sound of resistance.

The point being made here has nothing to do with Roman Catholicism. Laughter seeks out those in power. And if power bites back against laughter, then we begin to glimpse the grim face of absolute control – which is why the divine, above all, must have a sense of humour.

The decision to withdraw *Popetown* suggests a religion that cannot laugh at itself, a religion of claustrophobic disapproval, a religion where control is smuggled in under the guise of sensitivity. OK, sometimes the laughter is cruel – but there are bigger issues at stake. For the ability to laugh at oneself is perhaps the most effective litmus test which detects healthy from dangerous religion.

Elijah mocked the prophets of Baal for the impotence of their gods. He sarcastically lays into their lifeless divinity: perhaps 'he is meditating, or he has wandered away, or he is on a journey, or he is asleep and must be awakened'. It's not side-splitting stuff, admittedly. But it suggests a scriptural licence for having a go at some contemporary idols of thought. Christians can't stop the laughter. And we shouldn't want to. For we really ought to be laughing back.

Evangelicals have become this century's witch burners

The *Guardian*, 14 July 2003

Evangelicals may have won the battle over Jeffrey John's appointment to Reading, but many of those attending the General Synod at York are waking up to a deeper problem: the word evangelical is now firmly linked in the public imagination with intolerance and bigotry.

How did it come to this? In the late 18th and early 19th centuries the evangelical movement had a reasonable claim to be the social conscience of the nation. Evangelical Christianity was behind Wilberforce's successful campaign to abolish slavery. Elizabeth Fry and John Howard fought for prison reform and Lord Shaftesbury put a stop to children being sent down mines and up chimneys. It was a tradition that influenced many of the founders of the Labour Party and trades union movement.

Evangelicals define themselves by a love of the Bible. It is thus a tragedy for all Christians that they are now seen as the nasty party. Indeed, some moderate evangelical churches have become so concerned about the association between 'evangelical' and a narrow theological chauvinism that they are thinking of dropping the word. They are right to be worried, for in recent years a virulent form of right-wing Christian fundamentalism has infiltrated the evangelical movement. And they are obsessed with gay sex.

Many protest at the description homophobic – though anyone still in doubt that prejudice of the most disgraceful kind is at work here ought to visit www.godhatesfags.com. The arguments and biblical references found there are those used by evangelicals who mask their hatred behind that helpful Christian smile.

The contortions some will resort to in order to keep their denunciations of gay sex alive are astonishing. When the Archbishop of Canterbury, Rowan Williams, suggested that the Church might change its mind on homosexuality just as it had on slavery, the evangelical *English Churchman* hit back with an editorial justifying slavery as 'a form of social security for which many starving people today would be grateful'. One diocesan bishop apparently believes that homosexuality is caused by demons in the anus. Some single clergy have received excrement through their letterboxes.

In 1988 the decidedly liberal archbishop, Robert Runcie, addressed the third National Evangelical Anglican Congress – the most significant gathering of evangelicals on the calendar. He received a standing ovation when he called on evangelicals to integrate more fully into the life of the Church of England, insisting they must think of it as more than 'a convenient ship from which to fish for souls'. Church politics surrounding NEAC 4, to be held this September, show how far evangelical Christianity has shifted to the right since then. Under pressure from extremists, the NEAC leadership has withdrawn the archbishop's invitation to speak; instead, he will say the opening prayers. Even this is too much for some. 'In the light of the invitation to Dr Williams we can no longer commend NEAC 4,' concluded Reform, one of the most poisonous of the evangelical pressure groups.

Organizations like Reform have become a kind of Militant Tendency within the C of E, and the Church faces a huge struggle to free itself from them. Like Militant, they represent a tiny proportion of opinion. Only 33 churches are signed up to

Reform, out of 16,000 in the C of E, though some of them, like St Helen's, Bishopsgate, in the City of London, are extremely rich.

It was a small number of Reform churches which threatened to declare UDI from the diocese of Oxford over Jeffrey John's appointment (particularly St Ebbes, Oxford and Greyfriars, Reading). These same churches have been trying to blackmail the C of E into adopting their sub-Calvinist theology by withholding or capping their financial contribution to the central fund, which supports poorer parishes.

Unfortunately, most bishops have tended to the view that they could be accommodated into the mainstream by gentle persuasion and carefully crafted compromise. Unity in diversity has always been the C of E's signature tune, but these groups are singing a very different song. 'What a fresh start we would have if the Church of England returned to the Bible as understood in its historic statements. What a glorious prospect for revival there would be if she was rid of the liberals and Anglo-Catholics and pseudo-evangelicals,' the *English Churchman* concludes.

Just as Militant did of the Labour movement, groups like Reform and the *English Churchman* believe they represent the true voice of Anglicanism as expressed in the 39 Articles of Religion and the Book of Common Prayer. What they really want is a return to the Anglican Church of the 16th century. It's a world of anti-Catholicism and heresy trials: what has been done to my friend Jeffrey John is the modern equivalent of burning witches and heretics.

The Church of England was born in 1534 with the Act of Supremacy, the same year an act was introduced against 'the detestable and abominable vice of buggery'. This was also a sordid piece of politics by Henry VIII to leverage monks out of their valuable monasteries. It is an ominous precedent. The talk in the bars of the University of York, where Synod is meeting, is of a land-grab by evangelicals in advance of a possible split in the Church. Clearly, part of the attraction of the C of E to the likes of Reform is its historic assets.

Already some evangelical groups are preparing for a parting

of the ways. The misleadingly named Anglican Mainstream is setting up the infrastructure for an alternative worldwide Anglican communion. Those who delude themselves that religious fundamentalism only grows in very hot countries must wake up to the fact that it is getting extremely hot here.

I watched broken-hearted as Peter Tatchell and his friends invaded the Synod chamber on Saturday. I don't really care for his brazen self-righteousness (perhaps it is uncomfortably close to my own). Nevertheless, there was very little in his sermon with which I could disagree. Some members jeered and gave him the slow handclap. Many walked out. Press officers tried unsuccessfully to clear the press gallery. But most members stayed and listened – including, until right at the end, both archbishops. A small number gave Tatchell a standing ovation.

On Sunday we met in York Minster for worship. We sang: 'For the love of God is broader than the measure of man's mind; and the heart of the Eternal is most wonderfully kind. But we make his love too narrow with false limits of our own, and we magnify his strictness with a zeal he will not own.' There had to be a rehearsal for this hymn. Apparently, some people didn't know it.

You know what I find obscene?

Church Times, 26 November 2004

For the last two years, ABC television in the United States has shown *Saving Private Ryan* on Veterans Day. It's a great film. This year, however, 66 ABC affiliated stations refused to show it. The stations had come under pressure from the American Family Association and Christian conservatives because the film was seen as too violent and because there is too much swearing in it.

What sort of madness has descended upon America in the name of 'values'? I wager these same groups were not out protesting about the hundreds of people being killed in Iraq or the US soldier who shot a wounded unarmed man lying on the floor of a Fallujiah mosque.

It is precisely this sort of hypocrisy and narrow-mindedness that is attacked in that other great war film, *Apocalypse Now*: 'I taught young men to drop fire on women and children,' says Colonel Kurtz, 'but they were not allowed to write the word "fuck" on their aircraft because the army considered that to be obscene.' Which, in my book, is a very rough and earthy rendition of Matthew 23.27: 'Woe to you, scribes and Pharisees, hypocrites! For you are like whitewashed tombs, which on the outside look beautiful, but inside they are full of the bones of the dead and all kinds of filth.'

All of which is a warning against confusing Christianity with wholesomeness. Yet it is this very confusion that has taken root in the popular imagination. In terms of domestic policy, Christianity is a religion of sentimental pastel shades and family values. It is a religion of clean living virtue and simple homespun certainties. In terms of foreign policy, Christianity is red in tooth and claw. After all, all this virtue needs defending – and by whatever means possible.

In fact, it is precisely the sense of its own virtue that provides America with a narrative in which it is perfectly justifiable for it to have WMD and an interventionist foreign policy while expressing horror that other countries have the same. In other words, America too often uses Christianity as a moral alibi for doing what it likes.

The truth is, there is not very much in the Bible about family values. Indeed, Jesus says much that is critical of the family, preferring the extended family of the kingdom. There is, however, a great deal about poverty, how one treats the outsider and the alien, about warfare and forgiveness. 'Woe to you, for you tithe mint, dill and cumin, but neglect the weightier matters of the law: justice and mercy and faith.'

The idolatry of holy books

The *Guardian*, 17 August 2005

Salman Rushdie has now joined those who insist that Islam needs a reformation. What better place to assess such a demand than in the new Musée International de la Réforme in Geneva? Here familiar portraits of Luther and Calvin magically appear in a mirror to lip-sync the glories of the 16th-century Reformation – a revolution against a corrupt Catholic Church that ripped off the gullible by selling passports to heaven. By translating the Bible into the vernacular (one of the earliest and most influential English Bibles was produced in Geneva in 1560), the reformers bypassed the power of the Catholic clergy to interpret the word of God to ordinary believers. The parallels with a religion that refuses to accept the authenticity of translations of the Qur'an are superficially powerful.

Even so, Islam already resembles a reformed religion a great deal more than Rushdie acknowledges. Reformation pamphleteers railed against the papacy as the whore of Babylon, yet there is no equivalent centralized authority in Islam. Nor is there a hierarchical clerical establishment. The sober dress of Muslim leaders and the absence of fancy vestments to mark them out as special are clearly reminiscent of post-Reformation austerity.

So too is the thoroughgoing commitment to iconoclasm. On 6 August the *Independent*'s front page lamented what it called 'The destruction of Mecca'. 'Historic Mecca, the cradle of Islam, is being buried in an unprecedented onslaught by religious zealots,' it explained. The newspaper cast Muslim iconoclasts as philistines mindlessly destroying their own culture. In fact there is nothing 'unprecedented' about religious iconoclasm, nor is it always an act of unthinking fundamentalism. Iconoclasm is at the heart of the Abrahamic faiths and is as old as the Ten Commandments. Long before Marxists such as Georg Lukacs started warning about reification – turning something living into a thing or commodity – the Abrahamic faiths knew that God necessarily remains beyond the reach of human formulation and therefore sharp and circumscribed descriptions are bound to mislead. Making God into some sort of thing, giving God a definite shape and category, is to supplant the essentially mysterious with a dangerous human fabrication, a golden calf.

The moral of iconoclasm is that we must distrust our images, even our treasured mental images, of the divine, which is why iconoclasm can never be simply the preserve of the religious zealot destroying graven images.

The reformers didn't smash stained-glass windows as an act of cultural vandalism: they wanted to warn against falling in love with our images of God – infused as they are with our own political and social agendas – rather than with the utterly mysterious God who can never be captured in paint or statue or concrete. Applying this same logic to religious texts is the beginning of a much-needed modesty within religious conviction. No true iconoclast could ever believe he knew God's mind sufficiently to plant a bomb on a tube.

But the problem with the reformers is that they never came to appreciate that texts require iconoclastic deconstruction. Like most reformed churches, the cathedral in Geneva places the Bible at the dramatic centre of the building. What the reformed traditions often don't get is that they have given up worshipping images only to worship a book. At this point Salman Rushdie's call for a reformed Islam dangerously reinforces the tendency for religions such as Christianity and Islam to make a fetish of the written word – presumably hardly Rushdie's intention at all.

For there can be few more chilling examples of theocratic fascism than Calvin's Geneva. In toppling the authority of the clergy, he made it the responsibility of the civil magistrates to enforce the word of God. Spon, in his *History of Geneva*, writes: 'In the year 1560, a citizen [of Geneva], having been condemned to the lash by the small council, for the crime of adultery, appealed from its sentence to the Two Hundred. His case was reconsidered, and the council, knowing that he had before committed the offence, and been against caught therein, condemned him to death, to the great astonishment of the criminal.' Elsewhere, Picot observes: 'There were children publicly scourged, and hung, for having called their mother she-devil and thief. When the child had not attained the age of reason, they hung him by the armpits, to manifest that he deserved death.' Quite clearly, the fear that western liberals have of sharia law can hardly be appeased with reference to a reformed polity.

Rushdie's suggestion that a reformed Islam might find a way beyond the besetting sins of anti-semitism, sexism and homophobia is also, alas, unlikely. Luther himself was famously and virulently anti-semitic. The Reformation did little for women, and the place to find the most neanderthal religious homophobia in Britain today is in an organization called Reform. Until the Reformation finishes its work and trains its powerful commitment to iconoclasm on the sources of its own prejudice it will hardly be a model to hold up for other religious traditions to follow.

Rushdie should swap his crusading for novel writing

The *Guardian*, 21 September 2005

'In lending himself to the role of public figure, the novelist endangers his work; it risks being considered a mere appendage to his actions, to his declarations, to his statements of a position.' So argued the Czech novelist Milan Kundera, picking up the Jerusalem Prize for Literature in 1985. It's a piece of advice that another great novelist, Salman Rushdie, ought to ponder when he shifts into the writing voice of the columnist.

Over the last weeks, Rushdie the columnist has accelerated a debate that diagnoses Islam as morally sick and asks what medicine is needed to heal its ills. In his first attempt he offered the Reformation as the answer to what he calls 'mosque-based, faith-determined, radical Islam' (though I scratch my head as to why faith-determined is deemed a suitable criticism of a religion). In these pages I had a go at Rushdie's appeal to the Reformation as simplistic, arguing that reforming zeal often leads to the sort of bad religion of which he rightly complains. Taking the point, he has now changed tack: 'Not so much a reformation, as several people said in response to my first piece, as an Enlightenment. Very well then: let there be light.'

But this won't do either. Certainly Enlightenment thought offers a challenge to the moral poison that often oozes from superstition. Even so, secular rationality is no fail-safe prophylactic against murderous ideology. The 20th century offered up enough genocidal 'isms' to make that point. Hatred has the capacity to nestle within the most enlightened breast. So far, so obvious. But what's apparently not so obvious to Rushdie is that the most effective answer to bad religion is under his very nose: the novel itself.

The genius of the novel, according to Kundera, is that it is able to accommodate multiple moral universes, each interacting with the other, without the need to subjugate any one of them to some all-encompassing conclusion. The novel is pluralism in action. As Kundera puts it: the novel is 'the imaginary paradise ... where no one possesses the truth, neither Anna nor Karenin, but where everyone has the right to be understood, both Anna and Karenin'.

Admittedly, Kundera's advice was uttered pre-9/11. But these dangerous times require the moral imagination of the novel as much as ever. And this in two specific respects: first, in the capacity of the novel to be more humble than the pamphleteer with regard to ideology; and second, in its capacity to listen to and be affected by moral worlds very different from one's own.

Picking up an old Jewish proverb, 'Man thinks, God laughs', Kundera proposes that the novel was born out of the laughter of God. What's God laughing at? At the hubris of human attempts to deliver a single knockdown answer to the problems of the world. The novel can never be a cheerleader for Islam or Christianity or Modernist or Enlightenment. Those who believe that the exclusive truth of any of these is obvious and self-evident can never have heard the laughter of God.

But more important still, the novel has the rare capacity to nudge us out of our ideological trenches into a more sympathetic engagement with the moral universe of those we consider the enemy. 'When Tolstoy sketched the first draft of *Anna Karenina*, Anna was a most unsympathetic woman, and her tragic end was entirely deserved and justified. The final version of this novel is very different, but I do not believe that Tolstoy had revised his moral ideas in the meantime; I would say, rather, that in the course of writing he was listening to another voice than that of his personal moral conviction. He was listening to what I would call the wisdom of the novel.'

Columnists are often too busy attacking their opponents to make the time to inhabit their space. Mea culpa. It's a failing in a priest, but even more so in a novelist. Back in 1990, in that famous lecture that had to be ventriloquized by Harold Pinter, Rushdie laid out the vocation of the novelist as resisting the 'true believer . . . who knows that he is simply right and you are wrong'. The novel is a sacred space where all voices need to be heard. Which is why he proposed that even 'the most secular of authors ought to be capable of presenting a sympathetic portrait of a devout believer'. This is something Rushdie now seems increasingly incapable of achieving. He has become a true believer himself.

The tragedy is that Rushdie the novelist has increasingly been overtaken by his public crusading. The vocation of the novelist is to pluralism. That's why the novel is sacred. Unfortunately, it's a sanctity in which Rushdie now seems to have lost his faith.

Chapter 6

Atheism

Parasites on religion

The *Guardian*, 23 August 2002

What, I wonder, do the National Secular Society or the British Humanist Association have to say about the death of Holly Wells and Jessica Chapman? Not that I am after an explanation, for there is none. It is unfair, of course, to ask campaigning atheistic organizations such as these to answer the unanswerable. Nothing can be said to lessen the pain. Nothing can be said to explain why.

The vicar of Soham likewise has offered neither explanation, nor cheap comfort. But in his sermon on Sunday he drew upon a language that has taken the weight of human pain for generations. What equivalent language would secularists draw upon, and could it take the strain such horror and desperate sadness places upon it? What place would secularists invite us to go so that we might light our candles? And what would they say on Thought for the Day?

Why, indeed, do humanist groups want to associate themselves with a radio item concerned with religious belief in the first place? The reason is that the humanist agenda is almost entirely parasitic upon religious belief itself – humanists are largely defined by what they are against. And thus they are forced to follow religious groups around wherever they go. Contrary to expectations, it's not the case that humanist groups flourish as religious belief declines, it is the other way around.

It's a catch-22 situation: the more religion dwindles, the less interest there is in humanism. Hence the decline of humanism throughout the 20th century. We haven't gone from being a culture that believes in God to one that doesn't. We have become a culture that, for the most part, couldn't care less either way. Humanists fool themselves if they think this indifference is a vote for atheism, just as the Church fools itself by claiming a widespread (but untapped) spiritual yearning among the population at large.

The nearest thing the National Secular Society has to a positive creed is its declared aim 'to be on the side of all humanity, the side of intelligence, rationality and decency'. The British Humanist Association believes in 'an approach to life based on humanity and reason'. This is all very well, though about as informative as declaring oneself in favour of good things and against bad. The challenge is to make humanism something more than reactive or unobjectionably inane. The task must be not simply to attack religious belief but to defend and expound what the author Philip Pullman has called 'a big story' of its own.

As Rowan Williams, incoming Archbishop of Canterbury, has recently argued, a vision of human life that remains incorrigibly suspicious of all mention of the intangible ends up reducing social performance to the functional and instrumental – to 'managerial considerations'. It's the social and political equivalent of reducing 'I love you' to the chemistry of my brain.

The problem with militant secularism is not so much that it is anti-religious, but that in its desire to eliminate the religious instinct it closes off any sense of an explanation out of reach. It refuses the idea that there is something important about human life that we are unable to articulate, something that can only be said by the lighting of a candle. This need for the intangible is expressed when we feel our words fail us, when we try to describe the horror of a child's death or the beauty of a mountain top. It is in this context that the secularist reference to 'reason' or 'humanity' looks so hopelessly impoverished.

Pullman gives us a richly textured secularism in as much as he cleverly invokes a sense of otherness through the invention of fictional 'other worlds' and the idea of 'dust' (a case of having your cake and eating it, perhaps). Like much religious philosophy, these ideas fall apart when subjected to pressure. But the failure of religious philosophy is not the same as the failure of religion. Indeed, this failure is to be expected if the religious sensibility is really about what theologian Thomas Merton has called 'raids on the unspeakable'.

Pullman's sensitivity to otherness is rare among humanists and sharply in contrast to that of Oxford science don, Richard Dawkins, for whom the universe is nothing more than one big, complex biological/physical machine, the rules of which need simply to be learned and mastered. This is a closed language with no outside. It's a language that chimes with the propositional logic of the workplace, the language of league tables and utilitarian calculation. But what sort of language is it to offer those living though the ground zero of all hope?

The sorry state of contemporary atheism

The *Guardian*, 22 October 2005

Guess who said this: 'How much boundlessly stupid naivety is there in the scholar's belief in his superiority, in the good conscience of his tolerance, in the simple, unsuspecting certainty with which his instincts treat the religious man as inferior and a lower type which he has himself evolved above and beyond.' Some uppity Christian complaining about warmed-up anticlericalism in the Guardian? Or the most vociferous atheist of them all, that great genius of anti-Christianity, Friedrich Nietzsche. For although Nietzsche hated Christianity, he also recognized that atheism is prone to a self-satisfied smugness in which religion is written off as a fool's game, practised by suckers and easily co-opted by the wicked.

We hear a lot about the moral failings of religion, mostly Christianity. That's no bad thing – Christianity has been responsible for some of the worst moral outrages of western history. Those who dislike religion provide a much-needed counterweight, holding the faithful to account. But religions like Christianity are not without deep resources of self-criticism. Jesus himself was a fierce opponent of pathological religion and keen to expose its abuses of power. As Marx recognized, much of the critical apparatus of western thought was developed as a critique of Christianity – and mostly by Christians themselves.

But what resources of self-criticism has atheism developed? Little, it seems. Rarely is a critical lens directed inwards. Once the campaigning atheist has seen the light, they remain on-message, keen to convert all unbelievers. Last week, as Maryam Namazie picked up her award for Secularist of the Year, she proposed 'an uncompromising and shamelessly aggressive demand for secularism. Today, more than ever, we are in need of the complete de-religionization of society.'

Howard Thompson, former editor of the *Texas Atheist*, once insisted that: 'Total victory is the only acceptable goal in a mind-control war, because humanity is diminished so long as a single mind remains trapped in superstition.' This chilling certainty may be why modern-day campaigning atheists have lost much of the moral sophistication of their forebears. While the ordinary atheist remains indifferent to religion and all its ways, the born-again atheist has adopted the worst arrogance of Christian fundamentalists – just in negative.

Part of the problem is that many born-again atheists remain trapped in a 19th-century time warp, reheating the standard refutations of religious belief based on a form of rationalism that harks back to an era of fob-watches and long sideburns. One Oxford don has called the website of the National Secular Society a 'museum of modernity, untroubled by the awkward rise of postmodernity'. Ignoring the fact that at least three generations of thought have challenged an uncritical faith in rationality, the society continues to build its temples to reason, deaf to claims that it is building on sand.

This commitment to Victorian philosophy turns to farce when campaigning secularists describe themselves as freethinkers. In truth, atheism is about as alternative as Rod Stewart. The joke is that many who were converted at university via Richard Dawkins's *The Selfish Gene* think of themselves as agents of some subversive counterculturalism. This is ridiculous to Da Vinci Code proportions. Contemporary atheism is mainstream stuff. As John Updike put it: 'Among the repulsions of atheism for me has been its drastic uninterestingness as an intellectual position.'

Philosophers of the calibre of Nietzsche made the effort to understand what animates genuine religious belief – which is why his attack upon Christianity is all the more effective. These days, philosophical acumen has been replaced by cheap jokes about the sexuality of nuns. As religion returns to the geopolitical scene with frightening malevolence, secularists ought not to be handing out awards and congratulating themselves. They must first try to understand religious belief. That means dispensing with their own self-congratulatory piety: it's the only route to an effective challenge.

Atheism can save us from childish ideas

Church Times, 19 March 2004

In his inaugural lecture as Norris-Hulse Professor of Divinity at the University of Cambridge, Denys Turner offered some advice on 'how to be an atheist'. The barefaced cheek of a Christian theologian encouraging atheists to raise their game in response to the complexity of the Christian tradition is wickedly funny and genuinely important. Too many atheists have become intellectually lazy and conceptually flat-footed in their denial of God's existence.

Take the recent contribution by the *Sunday Times* columnist Minette Marrin. Deriding the Archbishop of Canterbury's engagement with the brilliant children's author Philip Pullman (News, 12 March), she attacks Dr Williams's 'trendy opportunism'. Dr Williams quotes Simone Weil's idea of 'purification by atheism'. Ms Marrin retorts that 'this is simply incomprehensible to me'. She doesn't understand. Well, she's right about that.

She goes on: 'Those with specific religious beliefs tend, almost by definition, to be fundamentalists.' By describing Christianity as essentially 'fundamentalist', she makes it childishly easy to rubbish.

As Professor Turner points out: 'It is extraordinary how theologically conservative some atheists are, and one might even speculate that atheists of this species have an interest in resisting such renewals of the Christian faith as would require the renewal of their rejection of it.' Atheists like Ms Marrin hate Christians to believe anything other than the Sunday-school version of God, because it makes their job of denying God increasingly difficult. Many modern atheists can't cope with denying anything more sophisticated than an old man with a beard smiting unbelievers.

Professor Turner challenges atheists to grapple with Thomas Aquinas's insistence that believing in God is not the same as believing that a certain sort of thing exists. 'Suppose you were to count up all the things in the world on some lunatic project of counting, and suppose they come to the number n. Then I say 'Hold on, I am a theist and there is one being you haven't yet counted, and that is the being who created them all, God'; would I be right to say that now the sum total of things is $n + 1$? Emphatically no. God could not be both the creator of all things visible and invisible, and one of the things created.'

God is not an extra item on some imaginary list of 'things that exist in the universe'. To that extent, God is no sort of 'thing': God is not the proper name of some item that exists somewhere in the universe. Ms Marrin is not denying anything that traditional Christianity has ever properly believed.

This isn't 'trendy opportunism'; it's basic Christian doctrine. God is transcendent, and so beyond the reach of human definitions. If we trust in God, then Christians mustn't be afraid of atheism. Rather, we must thank atheists for leading us away from inadequate conceptions of the divine; hence 'purification'.

However, whereas Ms Marrin's atheism relies on a Sunday-school conception of God, the atheism of Philip Pullman's children's novels must be taken seriously. For Pullman, God is simply power, a malevolent authority that crushes the joy from human life. If this indeed is God, then I'm with Pullman. But a God of love would look very different, and that's the God that most of us believe in.

Chapter 7

Sex talk

Let's get naked

Thought for the Day, 21 July 2005

My friend Isobel wasn't in church last Sunday, as she often is. Instead she flew up to Newcastle to stand naked on the Quayside and, along with hundreds of others, be photographed by the American artist Spencer Tunick. The images he produced were quite extraordinary: lines of naked bodies, kneeling or lying in rows set in the context of the vast buildings and bridges of the Tyneside cityscape. Here was an essay on the vulnerability of the human condition. No longer protected by our various uniforms, the human form looks so much more fragile and dependent, so much more at the mercy of the brutalities of urban life.

The Church has historically been far too suspicious of nakedness, often leaping to the assumption that nakedness is always about sex. According to the book of Genesis, the shame of nakedness is the very first consequence of sin. But these photographs have nothing very much to do with sex and a great deal to do with our common humanity.

I don't suppose I'd have had the guts to take my kit off on a chilly Newcastle morning. But I also think my cowardice has kept me from an experience that could have been profound and transformative. For doing without rings and jewellery, dispensing with the status and social messages we communicate to each other through what we wear, offers us the chance to recognize each other afresh as fellow human beings, lumpy bits of pink and brown flesh, all in need of warmth and food and love. Perhaps the most remarkable claim of the Christian gospel is that this is what God looks like as well.

Spencer Tunick helps us to see a deeper beauty in human beings, a beauty that's got over the fact that we're not all Kate

Moss or Jude Law. Yes, the first impression is that people do come in the most extraordinary shapes and sizes. And some sights are more attractive than others. But soon enough all that smirking and comparing goes away. Soon it becomes apparent that what we really have in common is our fragility.

Right now, you might be putting on your make-up, hiding your bumps and blemishes with well-cut clothes, and working out what messages you want to give others through what you wear. This is the time of day that many of us arrange our masks and plan our strategies of concealment.

In contrast, within the Christian tradition, it is naked that we come before God to receive judgement. And it's easy to fear the gaze that penetrates our masks. 'O Lord you have searched me out and known me,' says the psalmist. 'Where can I flee from your presence.' Perhaps divine judgement is simply this: to be looked on naked, without defences, without excuses, with the eyes of a person who loves us. God or no God, how many of us can really cope with being seen like that?

The bullshit before the but

The *Guardian*, 20 June 2003

Everything before the but is bullshit. It's a useful hermeneutic rule when dealing with sentences of the type: 'I'm not racist, but . . .'. It's just as applicable to the official position of the Church of England concerning homosexuality: 'We're not homophobic, but . . .'. I'm not allowed to accuse others in the Church of homophobia, for it is one of the conditions of dialogue between people with 'different views' that we respect each other's viewpoint and don't call each other names. But if it looks like a dog and barks like a dog, by golly it is a dog. The Church of England is institutionally homophobic.

Moreover, my not being allowed to speak of homophobia in the Church is but a dimension of further scandal: the control that is being exercised by church authorities on those who do not believe gay sex to be sinful. Bishops are under huge pressure to abide by a form of collective responsibility on homosexuality, irrespective of their personal views. It's now a condition of appointment that bishops toe the line expressed in the 1991 document *Issues in Human Sexuality*: love the sinner, hate the sin. Except many don't think it a sin. What the bishops fear, of course, is rich suburban evangelical parishes withdrawing their financial contributions from already cash-strapped dioceses. Without these contributions, the ministry of the Church would not be viable in poorer areas. And so conservative parishes hold the Church to ransom over its theology.

The real battle isn't about Jeffrey John becoming the next Bishop of Reading. In reality, that's all over bar the shouting. The Bishop of Oxford, who appointed Jeffrey, took the church commissioners to court over the ethics of their investment policy and won. He's more than capable of standing up to the Taliban element in the Church of England.

More important is the battle looming over new anti-discrimination employment legislation coming from the EU. The Archbishop's Council has successfully lobbied the government to allow the Church an opt-out from this legislation so that any organization with a religious ethos can discriminate against homosexuals seeking employment. Yet as a joint committee of both houses of parliament has recently made clear, discrimination on the grounds of sexual orientation could apply to a caretaker at a church school or a secretary in the parish office. It is extremely likely that this exemption will end up being struck down in the European court.

The Archbishop's Council has been arguing that what is at stake is 'a fundamental question of the frontier between the law of the land and the internal discipline of churches and faith groups'. So, would it be acceptable for me to set up a religion that discriminated on the grounds of race and expect the courts to respect that? Of course not.

Moreover, for right or wrong, the Church of England is a part of the establishment of the state itself. Which means that the discrimination allowed to the Church of England reflects indirectly on the state. It's in this context that the recent letter by nine of the most conservative of the Church's bishops complaining at Jeffrey John's appointment can be seen as significant. Here the bullshit before the but is very interesting. 'We value, of course, the gift of same-sex friendship and if this relationship is one of companionship and sexual abstinence, then, we rejoice. We warmly commend such relationships to the Church as a whole.' If they really meant this they cannot now support legislation that discriminates on the grounds of sexual orientation, rather than sexual practice – which is precisely the way the legislation had been drafted.

If the bishops stuck to the logic of their position then they would have to 'rejoice' about cohabiting gay vicars – in the absence of any further information about what they do in the privacy of their bedrooms. Otherwise, *Issues in Human Sexuality* is a charter for ecclesiastical peeping toms. For the official line is that it is 'genital acts' that are proscribed. Setting aside the question of how the bishops ever know that 'genital acts' are going on in the vicarage, the adolescent in me knows that there is much fun to be had at first base and second base before one gets on to third base. So, again, asking these bishops to be true to their position means that holding hands and passionate kissing must also be acceptable. It seems an unexceptional theological principle that God made human beings for joy and not for misery. And there can be much joy in celibacy. But what these nine bishops miss is the idea that celibacy is a vocation, not a chastity belt for those deemed to have been born with an unacceptable sexual orientation. As Rowan Williams put it before he became Archbishop of Canterbury: 'Anyone who knows the complexities of the true celibate vocation would be the last to have any sympathy with the extraordinary idea that sexual orientation is an automatic pointer to the celibate life.'

The psychology of survival

Church Times, 10 September 2004

After his engagement at Greenbelt, the US biblical theologian Ched Myers has spent a week with us in Putney. During his talks, the penny dropped for me. After all this time thinking about homosexuality, I finally get why the Bible is apparently anti-gay.

The real obsession of the Hebrew Scriptures isn't about what people do in bed; that's a more modern fixation. What the Scriptures are really concerned with is children. Just as Yasser Arafat once said that his secret weapon was 'the Palestinian womb' (i.e. that the Palestinians are going to triumph through demographics), so, too, the people of ancient Israel were obsessed with their own survival. It makes sense.

It's how it all begins in Genesis – Noah being told by God to 'be fruitful and multiply', and Abram complaining that 'I continue childless', only to be blessed with descendants as numerous as the stars. It's why the Bible remains obsessed with barren wombs, eunuchs, and so on. What is going on here is the psychology and politics of survival – with the unproductive misrepresented at best as useless and at worst as traitors.

Mr Myers argues that too much of the biblical argument about inclusivity is played out over eunuchs. So, while the conservative Deuteronomy insists that 'No one whose testicles are crushed or whose penis is cut off shall be admitted to the assembly of the Lord' (23.1), the radically inclusive voice of third Isaiah sounds a different note.

'Do not let the eunuch say "I am just a dry tree." For thus says the Lord: To the eunuchs who keep my Sabbaths, and who choose the things that please me and hold fast to my covenant, I will give, in my house and within my walls, a monument and a name that is better than sons and daughters' (56.3–5). Note: *better* than sons and daughters.

Isn't this also the point of that otherwise baffling reading from Luke (14.26) that we had to squirm through on Sunday, about hating mothers and brothers and children for my sake? Mr Myers reasons that the challenge offered here is a head-on way of facing a family-obsessed culture with the full consequences of the gospel. This is a gospel where all are welcome to the feast, irrespective of wealth, gender, ethnicity, or ability to contribute to the population.

What an important reading it could be at a time when the gospel of good news to all is in danger of being smothered by a self-satisfied family-friendly exclusivism.

What we can do with anger

Church Times, 25 July 2003

I spent my time at the General Synod making mental notes of whom I would most like to push in the lake. What a satisfying way it would have been to leave the Church. 'Calm down,' says the voice of reason. No, I don't want to calm down and I don't want to be reasonable.

Many of my friends have left the Church because of its persecution of homosexuals. More than half of the group of us who did the degree course at theological college are now otherwise employed. Mike is a solicitor; Mark works in administration for the police; Robert is a university lab assistant. They were priests of real faith and sharp intelligence, who were disgracefully treated by the Church they served. Too right I'm angry.

But being like this is not good for my mental health. I'm not sleeping well and not concentrating on proper parish business. Neither is it good for my relationship with God. I can't say I'm very proud of myself. But what does one do with this degree of anger?

Into this emotional maelstrom, the archbishop has asked us to seek ways of recognizing each other as called by the same God and Father. That has to be right. Yet how do I come to see those who (to my mind) persecute gay and lesbian people as being called by God, rather than driven by prejudice? Or – less provocatively – how do I squint through my anger and begin to see God in others who (I assume) might not be squinting back?

It's nonsense to pretend that I can drop my anger as I can drop a ball. Small steps in the right direction are what I need to work on. I will have to spend time with my more liberal evangelical friends. I need to reclaim a sense that God is at work in the language they speak.

At the moment, I find it a language that sucks all the joy from the air. I need to revisit what we have in common. I need to find a way of expressing my regret at adding to division, while holding firm to the conviction that a huge injustice has been perpetrated.

It is when we feel like pushing people into the lake that our faith must make a difference. It's not about some counterproductive fake niceness; it's about a struggle to see what God sees in those we find impossible. Sometimes we see what God sees only when all our tempers have been shredded. For there is a reality to the present anger that is often absent from our theological posturing. It may be a reality that can lead us back to each other.

Love is the answer

The *Guardian*, 29 July 2005

'Civil partnerships are not a form of marriage,' the bishops of the Church of England have just asserted, nervously. Yeah, right. Imagine the scene: in front of a registrar and two witnesses, the happy couple will make binding commitments to each other, surrounded by their nearest and dearest. Tears will be shed, hands will be joined. And then off to the reception for a few glasses of pink champagne, followed by a lifetime of faithful love, companionship and sexual intimacy. Is this marriage?

Who cares what bishops think? They don't have a veto on our use of the word.

The bishops present themselves as the great defenders of marriage (though I have yet to understand how a gay couple getting hitched is a threat to my marriage). In reality, most are plain terrified of gay sex claiming a greater degree of moral validity and social acceptability. Many bishops want the image of homosexuality confined to public toilets – so much easier to condemn. Consequently, clergy have been forbidden from blessing civil partnerships. We can bless battleships, and cats and dogs at the pet service; just not gay couples wanting to commit to a lifelong relationship.

The Church may think of itself as the last bastion of family values and married life, but it was not always thus. The early Church often held a dim view of marriage, believing it to be a distinctly second-best arrangement for those not gifted with continency. Jerome sarcastically suggested that only men who were too afraid to sleep on their own ought to marry. Christians were to be the virgin brides of Christ.

Jesus himself was single and celibate – his greatest love being, apparently, a man – the mysteriously named 'disciple whom Jesus loved'. And even St Paul offers the reflection: 'It is good for a man not to marry.' This isn't a common text at wedding services. But there again, it's surprisingly difficult to find suitable texts. Many opt for the wedding at Cana of Galilee, on the assumption that because Jesus once went to a wedding, he must have been keen on them.

Yes, the writers of the New Testament did offer ad hominem support for marriage, but didn't provide a comprehensive theology of marriage for the simple reason that most didn't believe the world was going to be around long enough for that to matter. Hence St Paul's advice: if you are married already, fine – but don't make plans if you are not.

It's precisely this sense that the world is about to end that gives the New Testament its moral genius. It concentrates the mind on what's important. And their answer wasn't the institution of marriage – it was love. Whether within a marriage or in a civil partnership, it surely matters not: love and all its commitments, that's what counts. And when present, that's what will make a civil partnership holy.

Why you need love and more

Church Times, 5 August 2005

'Love is all you need', sing the Beatles. It's a great song, but is it true? After all, what they need in Niger is food and what they need in Palestine is justice. For such as these, the Beatles's love is a luxury affordable only by the comfortably off.

Which may be why there is an increasing reluctance to use the word love in theological debate. Speaking up for love is just like speaking up for good things and attacking bad things: so axiomatic as to be effectively contentless. Apparently, love is for teen magazines, not for serious-minded theologians. It's a wishy-washy concept that goes down well as a piece of engaging rhetoric, but easily falls apart under scrutiny. Furthermore, love has been so hijacked by Hollywood that it has come to mean little more than sexually charged emotional intensity. It's true: we live in a culture that has been submerged by bucket-loads of the most damaging and morally illiterate sentimentality.

All this said, it still shocked me that a lengthy statement from the House of Bishops on civil partnerships did not include the word love at all. Not once. What is at the heart of the debate about gay partnerships is the simple reality of two people in love. For many of us, gay couples ought to have the same opportunities to express that love – both physically and within the context of legal institutions that help cement faithful and stable relationships – as straight couples. The bishops may discuss sex in their statement. But in refusing to mention love, they divorce sex from the context of loving relatedness in such a way that it is bound to be seen as morally inadequate. The love that dare not speak its name isn't sex; it's love itself.

I partly blame Anders Nygren and his wrong-headed book

Agape and Eros. Following that book, Christians commonly trot out a simplistic distinction between a love that is selfless and caring – Agape – and that which is apparently self-seeking and appetitive – Eros. It's a false distinction that allows erotic love to be conveniently ignored or condemned. The love of God is passionate, personal and, in the person of Jesus, physical. God's love is both Agape and Eros.

During a wedding I conducted last Saturday, the best man read those familiar words: 'If I speak in the tongues of men and of angels but have not love I am a noisy gong or a clanging cymbal.' What better comment could there be than this on the House of Bishops' statement on civil partnerships?

The mad, bad world of Archbishop Peter Akinola

The *Guardian*, 19 November 2005

'I cannot think of how a man in his senses would be having a sexual relationship with another man. Even in the world of animals, dogs, cows, lions, we don't hear of such things.' 'God created two persons – male and female. Now the world of homosexuals has created a third – a homosexual, neither male nor female – a strange two-in-one human.' Welcome to the mad, bad world of Peter Jasper Akinola, like Jesus a former carpenter, now the Archbishop of Nigeria and ringleader of a clique of archbishops trying to unseat Rowan Williams from Canterbury.

In marked contrast to the previous generation of Anglican archbishops in Africa – Desmond Tutu and Walter Makhulu – Akinola has been cleverly exploiting cultural differences between the more liberal north and the more conservative south, particularly over homosexuality, as leverage in an unprecedented takeover bid for the Anglican franchise.

Just last month he made his most audacious move, rewriting

the Anglican Church of Nigeria's constitution to exclude all references to 'communion with the see of Canterbury' – the means by which Anglicanism has always been defined. And this week Williams received a poisonous letter, questioning his ability to lead the communion, from Akinola and an uncertain number of fellow archbishops (at least one of whom had his name added without his consent).

When Henry VIII invented the Church of England as a handy way of sorting out his messy social life, he could hardly have expected to be founding a denomination of Christianity that would come to have some 70 million adherents spread across the globe. During the 19th century, public schoolboy missionaries would ride alongside the armies of the British empire to plant Anglican theology throughout the globe. It proved a remarkably successful export. For while the mother church continues to shrink, African Anglicanism is rapidly expanding. In the 1970s there were 5 million Anglicans in Nigeria; there are now 18 million – and that figure is expected to double by 2025.

Such is their numerical success at home that their ambition has become global. For as the power in Christianity shifts from north to south, so Akinola is encouraging a new set of African missionaries to return what seems a claustrophobic and bullying version of the gospel back to the Godless north. Rowan Williams has warned the assembly of southern archbishops of 'crude, threatening proselytizing' – to which they came over all innocent with the reply: 'None of us would support such an approach during these critical times, and we wonder to whom you were referring?' Yet it remains Akinola's express aim to reverse the 'satanic attack' upon the Church by liberals such as me who believe sexuality, and gay sexuality no less, to be a gift from God.

Bridgeheads for the assault on the Church of England spring up almost daily. The deeply conservative retired vicar of Holy Trinity Brompton, the Revd Sandy Millar – he of Alpha Course fame, sometimes known as the vicar of Harrods – is to be made a bishop in the Church of Uganda. Yet, bizarrely, he will operate in London as an assistant bishop in the diocese of Kampala – a bit like an ecclesiastical version of an absentee landlord. An evangelical church in Wimbledon has recently brought in an unknown South African bishop because its own bishop is refusing to condemn civil partnerships for clergy. As Rowan Williams struggles with seemingly infinite Christian charity to hold it all together, Peter Akinola and his friends are out to break it apart and run off with the pieces.

So why aren't liberals fighting back? In a recent sermon, the Revd Canon Marilyn McCord Adams, regius professor of divinity at Oxford University, offers a view few are prepared to admit: 'One whispered reason why many personally convinced liberals do not act is "postcolonial guilt".

'I agree that colonial condescension – whether of the Victorian or the more recent economic variety – is a grievous sin. We were, and are, arrogant in promoting European culture as normative worldwide. True repentance does not come through role reversal, however, in which the oppressed get a turn to lord it over their former rulers. Our Church is not called to take its punishment by letting Archbishop Akinola make Nigeria normative for Europe and North America instead.

'When the Church of England takes responsibility for keeping the Anglican communion together, she is continuing to act as the ecclesial wing of a colonizing power, still shouldering "the white man's burden". The responsibility has become agonizing because she has conceded the authority to dictate policy to some of the former colonies who are turning it against others, perhaps even Mother Canterbury herself!'

It is observed, in Akinola's defence, that his real concern with a gay bishop in New Hampshire is that it lands a propaganda coup to Muslims keen to depict the Anglican Church as the bastard child of the sexually decadent west. Indeed one reason Rowan Williams is wary of expressing his own views on homosexuality is that he believes liberal pronouncements from Canterbury may translate into lives being put at risk in northern Nigeria, where Islam and Christianity are locked in an often violent struggle.

The former president of the Christian Association of Nigeria, Sunday Mbang, has commented that 'most of these people who kill people come to our churches'; that 'they will walk very holy and shout holy, holy, and you don't know them'. The tragedy is that while Rowan Williams keeps his own counsel, Akinola is playing a dangerous game of poker, trying to outbid fundamentalist Islam with fundamentalist Christianity.

What does all this matter? After all, the Anglican Communion is a product of western imperialism and impacts very little upon ordinary churchgoers in Britain. Who cares about the commonwealth at prayer? In fact, millions in Africa and Asia, and most of us in the Church of England, care a great deal. The Anglican Communion provides a vehicle through which smaller churches in often ignored parts of the world can have an international voice. These churches are well placed to become important structures through which the implementation of the millennium development goals is monitored. The fracturing of Anglicanism puts a huge network of aid, goodwill and mutual understanding at considerable risk. In a world dangerously divided by religious differences, Akinola's new-look Anglicanism is ready to create yet another fault line to set believers against each other.

Ironically, the person most optimistic about the future of the Anglican Communion turns out to be Gene Robinson, the gay Bishop of New Hampshire whose consecration sparked off this whole fight. Last week he told me: 'God is in charge and God is good. Therefore everything will be all right.' I guess Rowan Williams thinks something similar. I wish I had their faith.

Would you walk from a lynching?

Church Times, 27 January 2006

The Nigerian government has proposed to make it an offence punishable by five years' imprisonment for any citizen to take part in a gay civil partnership. The justice minister, Bayo Ojo, said the law would also ban 'any form of protest to press for rights or recognition' of homosexuals. Given that homosexuality is already illegal, and in some parts of Nigeria punishable by death, the question is why the government bothers with all of this.

I have just been reading the US state department's assessment of human rights in Nigeria (www.state.gov/g/drl/rls/hrrpt/ 2004). The election of President Olusegun Obasanjo was 'marred by serious irregularities and fraud, including political violence'. The report speaks of 'numerous human-rights abuses' and 'extrajudicial killings'; 'female genital mutilation remained widely practised and child abuse and child prostitution were common,' it says. This is a country that regularly comes near the top in polls of the most corrupt in the world. Nearly 100 million people live below the poverty line.

Attacking homosexuals is a convenient (and time-honoured) way of distracting attention from this misery. 'Such a tendency is clearly un-biblical, unnatural and definitely un-African,' President Obasanjo said of homosexuality to a conference of Nigerian bishops in October 2004. This is the man accused by the US state department of sanctioning politically motivated killings. So why are the bishops taking moral lessons from him?

Jim Naughton, the communications director for the diocese of Washington in the US, makes a good point on the Thinking Anglicans blog-site this week: 'I am always amused when Episcopalians who favour gay rights are portrayed by their ecclesial opponents as captives of their culture. Whereas the cultural influences of Nigerian society on Nigerian Anglicans are never acknowledged.'

Why is this stuff about homosexuality so important? Because, as I write, I imagine some poor bugger being kicked to death by a gang of thugs who say the Lord's Prayer every Sunday. I don't know for sure that it is happening. But I fear that it is.

If it is, then those who have created this storm of hatred and prejudice cannot defend themselves with the half-hearted excuse that violence wasn't the intention of their rhetoric. Whether from the Church or the government, attacks on homosexuality are easily heard as an invitation to thuggery. Nigerian gays are being stripped of basic rights. Protest is illegal. Forget the unity of the Church: not standing up to this is tantamount to walking away from a lynching.

Luther, love and Gloria Gaynor

The *Guardian*, 15 May 2004

'I did not love God and was indignant towards him, if not in wicked revolt, at least in silent blasphemy.' Martin Luther's admission that he had come to hate God sparked a theological revolution that transformed the political geography of Europe.

For Luther, service to a God who demanded human beings earn his love had become service to a heartless despot, impossible to please. The confessional had become a private hell of never being good enough, of never earning enough merit to satisfy the unattainable demands required for salvation.

Luther's deep sense of human inadequacy meant that a God who dealt with human beings strictly on the basis of merit was always going to be a God of punishment. He thus came to see his former understanding of Christianity as inherently abusive, as a destructive cycle in which the abused child constantly returns to the abusive heavenly father for comfort.

Parallels with arguments that are now transforming the political geography of Anglicanism are remarkable. For the debate about homosexuality is about a great deal more than sex. It is about the nature of God's love for human beings, and has much in common with debates that drove the Reformation.

The message the Church has given to gay Christians is the message Luther came to see as inherently abusive: God does not love you as you are – you need to be completely different before he will love you.

Take the Bishop of Chester Dr Peter Forster's advice that gay Christians should seek to 'reorientate themselves'. 'I would not set myself up as a medical specialist on the subject, that's in the area of psychiatric health,' he said. But gay Christians who have tried to become acceptable to God by subjecting themselves to electric shock therapy, or by being bombarded with pornography, have been forced into precisely the sort of private hell Luther experienced in the confessional.

Luther's theological breakthrough was to describe a wholly

non-abusive God, who loves his children gratuitously – not on the basis of merit. God's love is experienced as grace, freely given, not as a demand that, in order to be loved, human beings must become something impossibly different from what they already are. It was a conception that released Christians from bondage to a theological construction that made their lives seem as desperate as a hamster on a wheel.

Against those who would conscript this desperation into financial gain through the system of indulgences, Luther spoke of Christian freedom and the Babylonian captivity of the Church; against those who would make sexuality part of a package of guilt and self-disgust, he would renounce his monasticism by marrying a nun. Ecclesiastical authorities can no more insist on celibacy than 'forbid eating, drinking, the natural movement of the bowels or growing fat,' he declared.

Following Luther, generations of evangelicals described the joy of being released from the burden of impossible expectations. Remember Charles Wesley's hymn: 'I woke, the dungeon flamed with light, My chains fell off, my heart was free, I rose, went forth, and followed thee.' The next verse begins: 'No condemnation now I dread.'

Being saved is evangelical language for describing the new life beyond the censure of an abusive God – the sense of facing the truth, of admitting it to others, of being accepted as one is, of being released from the burden of impossible condemnation. Being saved is an experience emotionally identical to coming out of the closet.

This is not political correctness. It is about the nature of God. For the one thing all Christians believe about God is that he seeks to call us out of darkness into light, out of pain into joy, out of deceit into truth, out of oppression into freedom. Amazingly, Gloria Gaynor's gay anthem – 'I am what I am, and what I am needs no excuses' – turns out to be the contemporary voice of Luther's own protest: 'Here I am, I can do no other.'

Chapter 8

Individualism, for and against

We are all liberals now

Church Times, 24 October 2003

Imagine two sorts of community: let's call them thick and thin. The thick community is like an English village, or what a village used to be. Everybody knows everybody else's business. Back doors are kept unlocked. People are generally similar in their worldview. There remains a great deal of homesickness for this untroubled idyll.

The thin community, on the other hand, is more what you find in town. People don't know much about each other: different worldviews and lifestyles jostle alongside each other, leading to low levels of social solidarity. Compared to the uncomplicated certainties of the thick community, the thin community is a confusing and antagonistic jumble. Opponents call it 'post-modernism', though in places such as London there has always been difference, as commerce has sucked in people from all over the world.

The trouble with the thick community is that it doesn't easily accept difference. To be different is to be strange, sometimes even wicked. To be different is to be a witch or a weirdo. To be happily gay in a thick community is often all but impossible. So it is that many young gay men and women escape their little communities and make for the city. In the city, everybody is weird and everybody is different. In this thinner community, different accents and languages, different religious and cultural beliefs, rub up against each other and require a modus vivendi based not on unanimity but on peaceful coexistence.

Of course, this is not a town v. country issue any more. In Western Europe, almost every culture is getting thinner. It's a function of global capitalism and the rapid expansion of cheap communications technology. Even in a small village, you can order a curry, watch American sit-coms, trade shares on the Nikkei or surf the web.

Our increasing appreciation of the cultural diversity of the world is dissolving the conviction that our way is the only way. Whether we like the description or not, we are all liberals now. Theological and political conservatism plays on our angst of change, but has little to offer; other than retreat and nostalgia. In the name of economic liberalism, Margaret Thatcher destroyed the old-style Tory party of colonels and squires, just as Tony Blair has destroyed the centralism of state socialism. The old pieties have gone.

Similar forces are at work in the debates over the future of the Anglican Communion. Some feel a yearning for the cultural homogeneity that Anglicanism once had. But the only way for a community to be both thick and global is for it to be an empire. To go on defending the cultural and intellectual boundaries of an imaginary thick community will turn our theological leaders into 'bouncers', to borrow a word from Archbishop Walter Makhulu's sermon to Inclusivechurch last week.

Having a common mind is no longer the way of defining communion. You don't mend the net my making it tighter. Indeed, it's better to have a network than a net; a group linked by the desire to follow Christ in which diversity is celebrated, not feared and suppressed. The question is this: are we after the imposition of unanimity or peaceful coexistence? What do they sing in heaven: unison or harmony?

What's so wrong with choice?

Church Times, 3 February 2006

Again, this morning, my first conscious act was to disable the radio so as to save me from yet another New Labour minister droning on about choice. 'Choice' is a magic word for politicians. Everybody wants it. Nobody can speak against it. The debates about the NHS are all about patient choice; the debates about schools are all about parent choice. Even euthanasia is being presented as an issue of choice.

'Choice' has become political fairy dust that can be sprinkled over any argument to give it popular appeal. Ah, I hear some smart alec reply: even you, by turning off the radio, were exercising choice. One can't get away from that argument: it's everywhere.

The reason why many in the Church remain deeply uncomfortable about the ubiquity of 'choice' as a stand-in for other, richer moral notions is because it seems a part of a wider phenomenon of collapsing all moral considerations into economic ones. The paradigmatic instance of 'choice' is staring at the supermarket shelves, wondering which cornflakes to buy. Choosing generates a sense of empowerment – after all, I could choose Frosties or Coco Pops. It's down to me. I'm in charge. Except, of course, it's not really much of a choice. The Tesco buyer decides what I have in front of me.

Existentialists famously made the notion of choice the centrepiece of their philosophy. The primary distinction of humanity is its ability to choose. Jean-Paul Sartre would go as far as to say that what we are, our fundamental nature, is not fixed, but a subject of choice. This is another way of saying that we don't have a fundamental nature at all. That's what 'existence precedes essence' is all about. We can choose who we are. This used to mean deep students in black rollneck jumpers smoking Gauloises and musing about what to make of their lives. It now means I shop: therefore I am.

What the existentialists knew, of course, is that claiming choice is also claiming responsibility. And the reason existentialism is associated with nail-bitten youths is because choice is about responsibility, and therefore about the anxiety of making the right choices. Suddenly, it's all down to me.

Why did I turn off the radio in the morning? Because, as the ever-sanctimonious Patricia Hewitt bangs on about choice, she is making it my job to run the NHS properly. Thus it's my fault – not hers – if it fails. The other day, Ruth Kelly was telling me that it's my job to run schools. No wonder I want to crawl under the covers and go back to sleep.

Poverty is worse than inequality

Church Times, 26 May 2006

If you had to characterize the difference between the 1985 report *Faith in the City* and the 2006 report *Faithful Cities*, it would be that the former was concerned with poverty, whereas the latter is concerned with inequality. As *Faithful Cities* puts it, inequality is the 'litmus test of the moral adequacy of any society'.

I don't agree. It doesn't bother me that I don't have the income of David Beckham. I am comfortable enough. The differing wealth of the Fraser and Beckham households is an example of inequality of wealth, though it doesn't constitute a profound moral scandal. The fact that some people die of hunger, some have insufficient access to good health care and clean water, and some live without a home – that is the moral scandal.

It's tempting to think poverty and inequality are roughly the same thing, but they aren't. The type of strategy that one might adopt in order to eradicate poverty is likely to increase inequality. As socialist societies the world over have discovered, the sort of economic strategy that one might adopt to increase equality is one that might well lead to the poor getting poorer. I happen to think an increase in inequality is a price worth paying to see a decrease in poverty.

The only Anglican theologian I can think of who says such things is the Revd Dr Alan Billings, who, as it happens, was one of the authors of the original *Faith in the City*. Had the authors of this new report spoken to him, they would have heard him tell of the transformation of many of the deprived communities that the *Faith in the City* group visited back in the 1980s.

It's fair enough to note that flashy developments don't always help the poor. None the less, since the 1980s unemployment has been reduced radically, and the wealth of the poorest has increased significantly. There are still places where people are far too poor. But there are fewer of these places than there were 20 years ago.

The problem with this new report is that it says a great deal about the failings of the market economy, and very little about its advantages. Markets make jobs; they keep prices down; and they bring dynamism to our streets. London is, and always has been, a great big market. That is why people from all over the world have come here. It is the market that gives London its social and ethnic diversity. Unless the Church learns to come to terms with this reality, it will never fully appreciate what makes the city tick.

Waiting for Godot, not Benedict

Church Times, 29 April 2005

In 1836, Augustus Pugin produced a rant entitled: *Contrasts: or a Parallel between the Noble Edifices of the Middle Ages and Corresponding buildings of the Present Day; shewing the Present Decay of Taste*. According to Pugin, the English towns of the 1440s were obviously Christian – gothic spires, clean air, close-knit communities, and peasants happy with their lot. In contrast, the English towns of his day were places of smog, prisons, and capitalism, with not a church in sight. His message: English Christianity is essentially communal and medieval.

Last week, the Puginesque figure of the Bishop of London welcomed the new Pope by quoting, apparently with approval, from the celebrated final paragraph of Alasdair MacIntyre's *After Virtue* (Duckworth, 1981): 'What matters at this stage is the construction of local forms of community within which civility and intellectual and moral life can be sustained through the new dark ages which are already upon us . . . We are waiting not for a Godot, but for another – doubtless very different – St Benedict.'

In their different ways, Pugin, Professor MacIntyre, and many senior bishops and theologians in and around the C of E, particularly those influenced by radical orthodoxy, have this idea that, somewhere between the Reformation and the Enlightenment, things went badly wrong. Whether it's pre-Raphael, Duns Scotus or John Locke – ethically and theologically, things were better in some mythic past, when communities were small and strong, and before the birth of the ugly twins of liberalism and capitalism.

It's easy to be tempted by the communitarianism suggested by philosophers such as Professor MacIntyre. Setting itself up against a self-serving individualism, it seems to offer a Christian version of *Coronation Street*, where people congregate in the church, rather than the pub. But what gets forgotten in the celebration of faux medieval community is that this was an era of ecclesiastical authoritarianism and murderous religious intolerance, where power and superstition were fused – not least in the person of the Pope. The community imagined by the present-day friends of Pugin requires just this type of anti-liberal authoritarianism to keep it in place.

The word 'community' has an unrecognized shadow side (like its cousin 'folk' or 'volk') that often indicates a rolling back of fundamental freedoms – yes, individual freedoms – that we too readily take for granted. So, no, I'm not welcoming the prospect of another Benedict attempting to obliterate freedom in the name of morality and community. Protestant that I am, I'd rather wait for Godot.

Beware of the Borg

Church Times, 19 November 2004

My favourite *Star Trek* villain is the Borg, a collective consciousness that is constantly out to assimilate individual identity into its beehive-like whole. The Borg is not intrinsically ill-intentioned; it is part of its nature constantly to expand and control: 'We are the Borg. You will be assimilated. Your biological and technological distinctiveness will be added to our own. Resistance is futile.' The logic of the Borg is to collapse all individuality into itself.

Such is the popularity of *Star Trek* that the term 'Borg' has taken on a life of its own. For computer geeks – who are often fans of science fiction – those who use Microsoft software have been assimilated or 'Borged'.

Like all good science fiction, *Star Trek* plays on contemporary fears. In the case of the Borg, it's the fear of a political community in which individuality is annihilated in the service of the whole; the fear of communism or of being an insignificant cog in the wheels of multinational capitalism. It's the fear of being taken over by forces beyond one's control.

This brings me to the Windsor report. It strikes me that the report opens the door to a dangerously Borg-like Anglican Communion. 'A body is thus "autonomous" only in relation to others: autonomy exists in a relation with a wider community or system, of which the autonomous entity forms a part,' it asserts. Alongside such sentiments go an unquestioned valuation of community (good) and individuality (bad).

For a number of years now, theologians have been laying into the Enlightenment and the celebration of the individual that forms so central a part of Enlightenment philosophy. We have been persuaded to hear 'individual' as another word for selfishness. But, to those who have cause to defend their individuality against Borg-like political communities, the word 'individual' is another word for freedom – not the freedom of egocentric self-assertion, nor the freedom to shop, but the freedom from totalitarianism or collective control.

Recent Anglican theology has emphasized the sinfulness of the go-it-alone individual, only to become dangerously naive about the dangers of community and collectivism. Our Trinitarian theology has repeatedly emphasized the oneness of the three, but rarely the threeness of the one.

What lurks in the pages of the Windsor report is the prospect of a multinational religious conglomerate, into which individual Christians are called to dissolve themselves in the name of communion. 'We are the Borg. You will be assimilated.'

Trinity as relationship

Thought for the Day, 5 March 2005

Perhaps the best known philosophical sound bite is René Descartes' 'Cogito ergo sum', 'I think therefore I am'. What Descartes was trying to do was find some form of knowledge that it's absolutely impossible to doubt. We can doubt the existence of the outside world or the existence of other people, he argued. After all, we could be dreaming or some higher power could be misleading us. But it's not possible to doubt that, at the centre of everything, there is some 'me' doing the thinking or the doubting. Thus, Descartes concludes, the only thing we can know for sure is that I exist.

This reasoning has become a very influential trap for modern western thought. For in locating certainty within the individual, philosophers have found it fiendishly difficult to describe any sort of bridge that links my own personal reality to the reality of other people. So we become stranded within ourselves, the private self becomes some sort of prison, with the solitary 'I' caught deep within. Poets and writers have described this modern condition as one of alienation. They speak of our yearning to find a sense of reality that connects us back up with each other and the world in which we live.

Tomorrow is Mothering Sunday. Once we have cleared the decks of hype and sentimentality, we are left to reflect upon the simple intimacy of mother and child. Think about a mother breastfeeding her baby – this isn't two separate individuals desperately trying to infer the reality of each other. That's surely why Henry Moore often carved his Mother and Child sculptures out of a single piece of stone. No, the intimacy of the mother feeding her child suggests that the primary reality is not autonomous selves struggling to find each other, but rather that relationship exists prior to a sense of separate selfhood. Relationship, our fundamental connectedness: these things come first.

For Christian theologians, loving relatedness is the very heart of reality. It's what binds mother and child as one, just as it binds Father, Son and Holy Spirit as one. For the Trinity is not three separate units trying unconvincingly to squeeze into oneness. Rather, it's a way of saying that God is fundamentally relational. Simply put: God is the love that binds all things together. And if this is right, then we are not separate units struggling to make contact, but like the mother and child, we are carved from a single piece of stone.

God's been mugged

The *Guardian*, 6 June 2005

'Michaela Newton-Wright has a rewarding job in advertising and lots of friends – but something is missing in her life. Although she is not religious, Christian athlete Jonathan Edwards offers her the chance to sample four practices from different religions. What will she learn from her spiritual shopping trip? And will these experiences change her life?' So goes the blurb for Channel 4's *Spirituality Shopper* which begins this evening.

Spirituality has become the acceptable face of religion. It offers a language for the divine that dispenses with all the off-putting paraphernalia of priests and church. And it's not about believing in anything too specific, other than in some nebulous sense of otherness or presence. It offers God without dogma. Spirituality is just the sort of religion suitable for one of Michaela's dinner parties with her 'lots of friends'. It takes the exotic and esoteric aspects of religion and subtracts having to believe the impossible, having to sit next to difficult people on a

Sunday morning, and having to make any sort of commitment that might have long-term implications for her wallet or lifestyle. Yes, spirituality is religion that has been mugged by capitalism.

Of course, spirituality has been around for a very long time. With all its beads and symbols, ancient wisdom is part of the appeal to the spirituality shopper. Except what they take to be spirituality is a distinctly 20th-century invention. As Professor Denys Turner rightly pointed out: 'No mystics (at least before the present century) believed in or practised mysticism. They believed in and practised Christianity (or Judaism or Islam or Hinduism), that is religions that contained mystical elements as parts of a wider whole.'

Around the end of the 19th century the idea began to gain in popularity that there was a central core to all religious belief that, while overlaid by culturally specific ideas and practices, could be accessed directly by 'personal experience'. Experience became the Esperanto of the spiritual life. When, in 1905, William James published his highly influential *Varieties of Religious Experience*, the path was set towards regarding religion as essentially about having extraordinary experiences, analogous in many ways to aesthetic experience.

It's why nowadays the cultured spirituality shopper prefers the Rothko room of the cathedral-like Tate Modern. Walking past churches, synagogues and mosques, the denizens of sophistication seek enlightenment in silent contemplation of the brooding maroon and black shapes of high modernism.

So strong is the association between spirituality and 'religious experience' that it has become common for some of the great spiritual writers of the Christian past to be read as describing esoteric experiences when, in fact, they are virulently anti-experientialist. For popular writers such as Meister Eckhart or the author of the *Cloud of Unknowing*, the significance of the mystical dimension in theology lies precisely in its rejection of the idea that God can be the subject of direct experience.

Perhaps the most influential biblical text on the development of spirituality is the story of Moses ascending Mount Sinai to meet God. Far from experiencing God, the higher Moses climbs, the more the clouds come down and the less he is able to see. Yet reading the mystics from a post-20th-century perspective, the absence of experience is often twisted into its complete opposite: the experience of absence. Which sounds a lot like a description of what it is to sit in front of a Rothko.

The idea that spirituality represents some innate human aspiration to the ultimate is a piece of modern candyfloss that neatly accords with the desire to participate in religion without any of the demands it makes upon you. It's religion transformed into esoteric self-help for those 'with something missing' – could it be a Porsche, could it be a new man, could it be God? For the Christians of the early Church, spirituality – not that they would have called it that – was about the death of the old person and the emergence of a new identity modelled on that of Christ. It's not something that one can dip into or an intriguing and unusual fashion accessory for the person who has nearly everything.

The unavoidable contrast is between *Spirituality Shopper* and BBC2's *The Monastery*. The former offers religion as a subjective experience that fits around our desperate desire to defend our rights as a consumer. The latter describes religion as that place where our obligations to others are tracked by simplicity, constraint and duty. Without this, religion is nothing more than a last-gasp lucky dip for the feckless and the fickle.

Billie Piper liberalism

Church Times, 28 July 2006

You couldn't dream up a more unlikely combination than Billie Piper, Doctor Who's glamorous assistant, and the Revd Professor Oliver O'Donovan, regius professor of moral and pastoral theology at the University of Oxford.

I've just finished reading a 'web sermon' by the professor, posted recently on the Fulcrum website, entitled 'The failure of the liberal paradigm'. It is a contribution to the homosexuality debate, arguing that liberals have cast the argument in profoundly unhelpful terms. Furthermore, it is liberals rather than homosexuals who are responsible for the mess we're in. It's a demanding article that ought to be studied carefully. But I think it is wrong – and for interesting reasons.

The professor's case against liberalism is a familiar one. Liberals begin with a sunny and overly optimistic view of humanity, allied to a concept of human beings defined primarily by will. The argument goes on: because human beings are fundamentally good, on balance, the things they want will be primarily good. Therefore, the eradication of constraint comes to look like a moral obligation. Hence liberals have a high doctrine of human freedom. If it feels good, do it, as it were.

The argument is that Christian liberals have latterly offered a biblical gloss on this obsession with freedom by invoking the language of liberation, thus disguising philosophical voluntarism, which asserts the primacy of the will, with the clothing of the Exodus.

In 1998, Billie Piper topped the charts with the annoyingly catchy pop song 'Because we want to'. It may be evidence that my brain is corrupted by popular culture, but I found myself humming this song while reading this latest assault on liberalism.

The song begins: 'We can do anything we want, we can, we can. We can do anything we want.' It then sets up a dialogue between a disapproving adult and a free-spirited teenager. 'Why you gotta play that song so loud?' 'Because we want to, because we want to.' 'Why d'you always dance all night?' 'Because we want to, because we want to.'

This is what Professor O'Donovan and many others think that liberalism is all about. And this is why they hate it. It invariably casts authority as the enemy, believing that its own wilful witness to the truth comes as a struggle to break down the backwardness that is characteristic of institutions and authority (i.e. the Church) – hence the progressivism that goes with liberalism.

Worse still, liberalism has no argument to support its assault on tradition and authority, other than the inarticulate 'because

I want to'. Little wonder that many conclude that liberalism is the enemy of reason. Little wonder that they warn homosexual Christians not to welcome the support they get from liberals.

Such critics are correct that there is a species of liberalism that's a bit like this. They trace it back to Kant and Hobbes. I'll call it Billie Piper liberalism. As it happens, I agree with them that Billie Piper liberalism is as philosophically unsatisfactory as her song. But what they don't acknowledge is that there's a very different liberalism – associated with people such as Edmund Burke – that is rooted not in a rosy view of human beings, but in a much more suspicious one.

Burke would have just as much beef as these critics with voluntaristic self-assertive liberalism. Indeed, he attacked the liberal proponents of the French Revolution because they insisted on an empty and dangerous voluntarism.

Burke's suspicious liberalism begins from an acknowledgement of human fallenness. Moreover, he applies the idea of fallenness so much more widely than evangelicals such as Professor O'Donovan; for Burke believes that it is not just wilful individuals that are fallen, but also groups, institutions, political systems, theologies, and Churches.

Edmund Burke's famous political caution applies particularly to those who reform out of a burning sense of moral virtue. These people are especially dangerous when they are too confident in their own position, and not prepared to acknowledge the fallenness of their worldview.

Liberty is an important principle in so far as it protects human beings from those who are convinced they know best; those who are convinced they always know the truth. Liberal freedom is not wilful self-assertiveness: it is an insurance policy against dangerous bullies who believe they have God on their side.

What gives this form of liberalism such an affinity with Anglicanism is that it disavows a clear-eyed certainty about the truth, in the name of peaceful coexistence between those of very different theological persuasions – which is just what Richard Hooker was after. It's a point made brilliantly by Christopher Insole in *The Politics of Human Frailty: A Theological Defence of Political Liberalism* (SCM Press, 2004).

Edmund Burke put it like this: 'Perhaps truth may be better than peace. But as we have scarcely ever the same certainty in the one that we have in the other, I would, unless the truth were evident indeed, hold fast to peace, which has in her company charity, the highest of virtues.' If any sentiment can save the Anglican Communion, surely it's this.

Chapter 9

Jewish Christianity

The 614th commandment

Church Times, 17 October 2003

No recent thinker has got under my skin more than the Jewish philosopher Rabbi Emil Fackenheim, who died last month. With remarkable boldness, he added to the 613 command-ments in the Hebrew Scriptures a new 614th: thou shalt not grant Hitler posthumous victories.

To some, this new mitzvah became a theological rationale for the existence of the state of Israel. To others, it was a critique of the process of secularization, whereby Jews marry outside their faith, thus contributing to the eradication of Judaism as any-thing other than a vague cultural phenomenon.

I was brought up in a secular quasi-Jewish family, in which being Jewish meant gefilte fish, strong women and commitment to learning. We maintained a sense of emotional solidarity with our past, though the practices of the Jewish faith had long been abandoned. Some time during the past generation, the family stopped putting 'Jewish' in the religion box on hospital forms, and fell in line with the majority default position: 'C of E'. Our Judaism had suffered the death of a thousand cuts. Reading Fackenheim awoke me to its significance, though, by then, there was no reversing the process.

Earlier this year, my wife and I fell out over whether we ought to circumcise our baby son. For her, circumcision is cruel and unnecessary. How could I disagree? St Paul's insistence that the gospel cannot be confined to the circumcised was a revolution-ary move against tradition and towards radical inclusivity.

But Fackenheim wouldn't leave me alone. To put it at its most visceral: I married a Scandinavian girl and now have three beautiful children who look like extras from a Leni Riefenstahl propaganda film. It all fed the low-level guilt that is the background to my theological imagination. Have I sided with the persecutors against the persecuted?

These are more than autobiographical observations, for finding a way through this complex emotional thicket is partly what is required if we are to understand the politics of Israel. A desire to condemn its persecution of Palestinians and illegal occupation of their land must not blind us to the dense emotional texture upon which Israel is founded.

For Fackenheim, the Israeli state is the guarantor of Jewish identity. And few issues are more visceral than identity. Even with the critical distance offered by my Christianity, I have little ability to discern the layers of guilt, betrayal, anger and fear that shape my attitude to Israel. No wonder the politics seem so intractable. Goodbye, Emil Fackenheim. I will say Kaddish for you.

Weep not for post-modernism

Church Times, 12 August 2005

The current debate about security has made one thing clear: post-modernism – at least, post-modernist ethics – is dead.

For understandable reasons, post-modernism sought to articulate a moral vision that set ethics at the maximum possible distance from the use of violence. The problem with this is that when decisions have to be made about the appropriate use of force, of imprisonment, and so on, the ethics we have been taught by post-modernism are no use whatsoever.

Let me explain. According to the great and still under-appreciated philosopher Gillian Rose, post-modernism was essentially a reaction to the horrors of the Holocaust. What post-modernists argued was that modernist approaches to rationality and ethics were implicated in the horrors of Auschwitz.

Subsequently, the new ethics that post-modernists began to develop were concerned with an ethical language that could never again be regarded as an accomplice to genocide. This meant that any ethics of obligation and force – or, as Professor Rose would say, any ethics that concerned themselves with law – were rejected in favour of a more abstract language, which opened up beautiful and intriguing moral fantasies. These, unfortunately, failed to connect with the type of moral decision-making that was necessary when bombs were going off.

Yes, there is still something to be learnt from extended reflections on 'otherness': but I hazard a suggestion that the most important task for ethics is to judge when state violence – going to war or locking people up – is and is not appropriate. This is precisely the sort of discussion to which post-modernism has become allergic. Post-modernism absents ethics from the discussions that need to be had by the powerful, leaving them to be shaped by the forces of anger, revenge, and sectarianism.

In effect, the failure of post-modernity originates in its desire for innocence, for clean hands. The reality of moral decision-making – particularly for those in power – is that there are often circumstances in which no option is attractive: to silence the preachers of hatred, thus denying a fundamental freedom of speech; or to allow extremists to whip up dangerous sentiments that may lead to more bombs?

Those of us who do not have to make such decisions often succumb to a false innocence of moral superiority, carping at tough choices that others make in what Rowan Williams once called 'tragically constrained circumstances'. Post-modern ethics colluded in this fantasy – which is why I'll shed few tears for its demise.

Laughter in hell

Church Times, 16 December 2005

The Institute of Contemporary Arts organized a seminar last week on the work of the philosopher Gillian Rose, to mark the tenth anniversary of her death. The Archbishop of Canterbury did what he does best, delivering a warm and thoughtful account of why her work remains required reading.

Professor Rose's work is an encouragement to pay attention to the philosophical condition of human fallenness. Human beings are haunted by complexity, compromised by mixed motives, and debased by threads of complicity with cruelty and untruthfulness.

We constantly seek to represent ourselves with various fictions of our own innocence – the innocence of the activist, of the silent or prayerful, of the victim – thus failing to recognize that we all own shares in the ways of the world. This isn't so much a counsel of despair; rather, it's a more honest description of the space we inhabit, and in which we all have to work out how to be good and how best to love each other.

What is remarkable about Professor Rose's thought is its courage. Just as she was keen to insist that life should be enjoyed in defiance of the cancer that eventually overwhelmed her, so too she spoke of the work of love as still being possible within environments that seem so morally inhospitable. She was fond of quoting Silouan the Athonite: 'Keep your mind in hell, and despair not.'

One of the ways she thought it possible to manage this seemingly impossible challenge was through laughter. As it happens, Gillian Rose had a rather irritating laugh – a bit like a tipsy schoolgirl – but her observation is bang-on. Think of the humour of nurses or undertakers. Laughter wards off despair, and so becomes a necessary accomplice in enabling you to keep your mind in hell. Laughter is a necessary accomplice of truth-telling.

Professor Rose explores this phenomenon in her writing about Hegel. But the person who deserves the Nobel Prize for the comedic harrowing of hell is the genius stand-up comic Richard Pryor, who has just died.

He was born to a prostitute in a brothel, became a cocaine addict, attempted suicide, and in later life suffered from multiple sclerosis – yet he was one of the funniest men on the planet. Like the best comics, he allowed us to glimpse the real horror of the world indirectly by expressing it as laughter. He kept our mind in hell, yet without despair. May he rest in peace.

The smashing of the idols

The *Guardian*, 11 February 2006

'How did Britain – home to the iconoclasm of Milton, Marx and the Sex Pistols – allow book-burning and fatwas to be decreed openly, in the streets of south Yorkshire?' asked Tristram Hunt in the *New Statesman* last year. Interesting thing to ask. How come it's Milton, Marx and the Sex Pistols that get to be cast as the iconoclasts? After all, it's the Abrahamic faiths that invented iconoclasm. And it's the Islamic prohibition against images of the prophet that prompted the latest furore over these cartoons. It's Muslims and Jews who are surely the real iconoclasts.

Secular commentators have conceived this whole cartoon row as a debate about the limits of free speech. From the perspective of the Hebrew Bible, that would be to regard the issue in terms of the third of the ten commandments: 'You shall not make wrongful use of the name of the lord your God.' That is, the cartoons are a form of blasphemy.

On the other hand, iconoclasm – from the Greek *eikon*, image, and *klaein*, to break – finds its origins in the very different second commandment: 'You shall not make for yourself an idol, whether in the form of anything that is in the heaven above or the earth beneath.' Because God is so utterly inscrutable, all representations of the divine are futile. We can never know what God looks like. There can never be anything like a theological Madame Tussaud's. Moreover, any attempt to depict the divine is recognized as an attempt to control it, to collapse it within the dimensions of human wit, to requisition it as support for one particular way of making sense of the world. The destruction of images isn't cultural vandalism; it's a warning against making the divine a puppet of human aspiration.

As Moses ascends Mount Sinai to receive the ten command-ments he is depicted as journeying ever closer to God. Yet the higher he climbs, the more mist and darkness envelops him. Mystical writers called it the cloud of unknowing. God dwells in 'unapproachable light'. In contrast, those at the foot of the mountain are casting the golden calf, a precise depiction of just what they reckon God to be like. It's the sort of God that will stand still and look the part as religious rituals are spun around it. And because this representation has been fabricated accord-ing to human expectation, it will always look more like God than God does. The danger with idolatry is that it produces clear-eyed believers, convinced they're right and convinced they know what God is asking of them. Iconoclasm is the sometimes comic, sometimes violent insistence that we must be modest in our knowledge of the divine. Yet to unquestioning believers themselves, iconoclasm is easily confused with an attack upon God.

Most image destruction has been within the Christian tradi-tion, only because Christians have disagreed about representa-tion in a way that Jews and Muslims have not. Christian art began slowly, with even St Augustine asserting that 'God should be worshipped without an image'. Others argued that because God became human in the person of Jesus, Christians are provided with an assured image of the invisible God, there-fore Christian representational art is fully justified. It's an argument that has waged its way through the centuries: images created and images smashed. It exploded in the eighth century and again at the Reformation.

Again and again, theologians have warned against uncritical subordination to representations of God, power or authority. That's the unlikely link between the iconoclasm of Milton, Marx and the Sex Pistols and that of the Judeo-Islamic tradi-tion. And it's why a condemnation of the Danish cartoonists by those within other Abrahamic faiths, acting in solidarity with our Muslim brothers and sisters, is not quite so straight-forward. A faith tradition that is never offended is one that is never challenged to give itself the necessary critical scrutiny. Indeed, the tendency to create dangerous idols of the divine is primarily a sin of the religious, not a blasphemy of the irreligious.

Purim

Church Times, 1 April 2005

The soldier outside the Israeli Army's foreign press and public affairs unit was drop-dead gorgeous. You don't expect guards to be wearing a skimpy, fluffy pink bikini while on duty. Major Sharon Feingold, the head of the unit, was less revealing, offering the party line on the need for security. Outside her office, the squaddies were vigorously celebrating Purim. For the first time in years, Israelis have been out on the streets en masse for Purim, a testament to the improved security situation for them.

During Purim, Jews remember the story from the book of Esther in which the Jewish people are saved from the machinations of the evil minister Haman, who has plotted their destruction. Like the soldier in the bikini, Esther catches the eye of the king, and, after wining and dining him, pleads that her people be saved. She wins the argument, and those who have sought the annihilation of the Jews are themselves slaughtered (Esther 8.11).

In the middle of Jerusalem, I came across the ultra-Orthodox Jews boogying to an open-air disco. Elsewhere, children have a day off school, and flood into town wearing fancy dress.

The major argued that the Jewish people in Israel are still under threat and need saving. It's a case that the army has not made well, and I was astonished to discover that an internet connection was linked to her office only four months ago. What does that say about how interested the Israelis are in explaining themselves to the outside world?

The more persuasive case was to be found elsewhere. At Sha'arei Zadek hospital, I was shown CCTV footage taken at the entrance to the accident and emergency department a few minutes after a suicide-bomb attack. At one point, a medical orderly opens the back door of an ambulance to find his daughter inside. The former head of the A & E department was himself murdered by a suicide bomber the evening before his daughter's wedding. There is no argument but that such horror requires the military to defend its people – and, if that means a barrier, then so be it. The real question is where the barrier goes.

A mentality of fear, and a belief that the Bible offers Israelis the title deeds to Palestinian land feed continued Israeli expansion. Just last week, the international community condemned the construction of 3,000 new homes at Maale Adumin, the largest of the Israeli outposts, near Jerusalem, but in the West Bank. Back at the hospital, there is a recently installed mass decontamination facility, ready for a chemical or biological attack on Jerusalem.

Apocalypse soon

The *Guardian*, 9 June 2003

Just as new life is being breathed into the peace process, religious groups throughout the US are whipping up hostility to the road map. The aim of the Christian–Jewish 'interfaith Zionist leadership summit' held in Washington last month was 'to oppose rewarding murderous Palestinian terrorism with statehood'. Attending the conference were some of the most influential figures of the Christian right; behind them a whole infrastructure of churches, radio stations and bible college courses teaching 'middle-east history'.

Since the late 19th century, an increasing number of fundamentalists have come to believe that the second coming of Christ is bound up with the political geography of Israel. Forget about the pre-1967 boundaries; for them the boundaries that count are the ones shown on maps at the back of the Bible.

The acceptance of the state of Israel by the UN in 1949

brought much excitement to those who believed the second coming was being prepared for. A similar reaction greeted the Six Day war in 1967. The displacement of Palestinians mattered little compared with the fulfilment of biblical prophecy. Writing in *Christianity Today* immediately after the Six Day war, Billy Graham's father-in-law, Nelson Bell, claimed the fact that 'for the first time in more than 2,000 years Jerusalem is now completely in the hands of the Jews gives the student of the Bible a thrill and a renewed faith in its accuracy and validity'.

So as the international community withdrew its embassies after the war, and the UN passed resolution 242 condemning Israel's occupation of the West Bank, the International Christian Embassy was set up to show support for Israel. Since then the Christian right has staunchly opposed trading land for peace or any attempt to broker a settlement by power-sharing arrangements. The destruction of the al-Aqsa mosque continues to be sought after by both Christian and Jewish fundamentalists. US churches are encouraged to form links with Jewish settlers via email and to support them through fundraising.

Happy to have any friend it can get, the Israeli government has long since exploited its connections with far-right US Christian groups. While moderate Christians, such as the Palestinian Bishop of Jerusalem, cannot get to see Ariel Sharon despite repeated requests, the door is always open to southern Baptists and TV evangelists.

What is astonishing about this marriage of convenience is that their version of evangelical Christianity believes that biblical prophecy leads to Armageddon and finally to the conversion of the Jews to Christ. According to the most influential of the Christian Zionists, Hal Lindsey, the valley from Galilee to Eilat will flow with blood and '144,000 Jews would bow down before Jesus and be saved, but the rest of Jewry would perish in the mother of all holocausts'. These lunatic ravings would matter little were they not so influential. Lindsey's book, *The Late Great Planet Earth*, has sold nearly 20 million copies in English and another 30 million-plus worldwide.

Against this crazy theological background, an ideological battle is now being waged. Despite the fact that apocalyptic prophecy as read by the Christian right ends with another holocaust, some Israeli politicians and journalists are encouraging fundamentalists to stick by the implications of their narrative. In a recent column in the *Jerusalem Post*, Michael Freund called upon evangelical Christians to lobby against the pressure being put on George Bush by Tony Blair and Colin Powell. 'If Jesus were alive today,' he wrote, 'the US state department would likely criticize him for being a Jewish settler and an obstacle for peace.'

There are 45 million evangelicals in the US and they represent a crucial block vote for born-again Bush. It is therefore to his credit that he has resisted their pressure and managed to persuade Sharon to accept the peace plan. Perhaps Bush is able to take the evangelical vote for granted in much the same way as Blair is able to take the left's vote for granted: both have nowhere else to go.

Yet Bishop Riah Abu El-Assal of Jerusalem doesn't trust Bush. He thinks the combination of European impotence and the US's refusal to pressure Israelis into stopping building settlements means the plan is already dead in the water. 'It took them six days to occupy the Palestinian territories; they could get out in three,' he says. Bishop Riah has persuaded the World Council of Churches to call for sanctions on all products from the occupied territories.

The diocese of Jerusalem runs hospitals in Gaza and Nablus. It's in places like these that the real work of Christian ministry is conducted. By contrast, US evangelicals oppose the peace process and swarm into Iraq to convert its people to Jesus.

Is this the Promised Land?

Church Times, 8 April 2005

The Gush Etzion settlement block was an unusual place for an English priest to spend Easter. Up in the Judean hills between

Bethlehem and Hebron, the Gush is one of the most controversial of the Israeli settlements, situated deep within Palestinian territory. Rows of neat, well cared for properties belie the reality: this is precisely the sort of place where peace deals come to grief.

The mayor, Shaul Goldstein, was prepared to concede nothing: 'We are no longer playing the role of the wandering Jew. We are establishing our roots in the homeland that God gave to us.'

In this world, the expected patterns of political affiliation don't apply. Ariel Sharon and George Bush are seen as dangerous liberals who are out to get them. The community is bitterly opposed to the separation barrier, which leaves a number of the villages of the Gush on the Palestinian side.

The inhabitants are equally hostile to Mr Sharon's disengagement plan, which they believe is a betrayal of their fellow settlers in Gaza. This is not a place where there is much support for the two-state solution. As one resident put it: 'The Palestinians already have a state. It's called Jordan.'

Everyone in Israel seems to think that their situation is a David and Goliath one, and that they are the vulnerable David taking on the might of Goliath. The residents of the Gush show a map of the Middle East, in which Israel is surrounded by 22 Arab countries – which they read as one unit. Similarly, the Palestinians show a map of the area in which small strips of land are surrounded by the might of the Israeli military and supported by US dollars.

Around the Gush, Arabic road signs pointing to Palestinian villages have been erased by spray paint. Our host referred to Palestinian lands as 'godless'. The local rabbi has taken a huge amount of stick from locals for speaking up for Palestinian rights and for participating in peace talks. 'He shouldn't get involved in politics,' said Shani Simkovitz, who came originally from Brooklyn. The rabbi should be visiting the sick and burying the dead, she said.

The Gush felt like something from a Stephen King novel. The town is apparently normal: people are cheery and polite; their houses are clean; their streets are ordered. The residents come together to put on musicals. But something is terribly wrong. Polite conversations have a shockingly racist undercurrent. Fundraising events seek to raise $14,000 for a new watchtower. The school bus is bullet-proof. This can't be the Promised Land.

St George's day

Thought for the Day, 23 April 2005

Crusaders returning from the Holy Land brought back with them fantastic tales of a warrior saint who suddenly appeared at the sieges of Jerusalem and Antioch on a white charger. During the course of the middle ages, he became famous, as one writer put it, 'for dragon maintenance and virgin reclamation' – though he is now more likely to be celebrated on the football terraces or associated with the ideology of racist thugs. Little wonder many of us are just a bit embarrassed by England's patron saint, whose feast day is today.

But last year, on a visit to the West Bank, I discovered a very different St George. A few miles east of Bethlehem, close by the Israeli separation barrier, is the Palestinian village of Al Khadir. Al Khadir, I discovered, is the Arabic name for St George and is widely honoured throughout the Muslim world. My guide ushered me through a courtyard and into the dimly lit Orthodox Church of St George. Did I know that George was a Palestinian, he asked?

Before the Intifada, when travel was easier, Muslims and Christians would come together from miles around to make pilgrimage to Al Khadir. The village streets would be packed, lamb would be barbecued in the churchyard, and Christians and Muslims would sit and eat together.

Why did I never learn about this St George? I went to boarding school in a small market town some miles outside Leicester, where we are today. We wore black uniforms in mourning for the death of Queen Victoria and sang about England's green and pleasant land in chapel. I would often escape school and hitch a lift into Leicester itself. Here was another world, altogether more magical and intriguing. Here was bustle and colour, languages that I didn't understand and people from places I'd never heard of. To a young boy, it suggested a world so much bigger than the one I was learning about in the classroom, a world of so many possibilities and with so much to wonder at.

St George, as it turns out, is the patron saint of precisely this sort of cultural and ethnic diversity. After all, he is the patron saint of Genoa, Georgia, Catalonia, Armenia, and he originated either from Palestine or Turkey. The irony is that while many racists claim St George as the standard bearer of Anglo-Saxon superiority, the only thing that can be said with absolute certainty about St George is that he was not born in this country and that his legend emigrated here from the middle east.

The sort of hospitality I found at Al Khadir suggests a St George that welcomes those of different creeds and colour, a St George that can help us to slay the dragons of racial superiority and religious intolerance. Now that's the St George we need today.

My friend, Mordechai

Thought for the Day, 13 November 2004

On Thursday, Israeli police entered St George's Anglican Cathedral in Jerusalem and re-arrested Mordechai Vanunu. He had violated the terms of his release from prison by speaking to foreigners like me.

We met some months ago. He was sitting quietly on the second row of the cathedral. After 18 years in prison, he was well used to silence. As a visiting priest, I was asked to read the lesson: 'For there is nothing hidden, except to be disclosed; nor is anything secret, except to come to light.' An extraordinary text to be asked to read in front of a man who had exposed the existence of Israel's nuclear weapons programme to the world.

Mordechai and I shared a beer in the cathedral garden after evening prayer. We spoke of his conversion to Christianity in Australia, of his theology of non-violence, his admiration for Gandhi, and of his time in solitary confinement. Every day in prison he would repeat to himself the end of Romans chapter 8. It became a sort of mantra of resistance: 'I am convinced that neither death nor life . . . nor rulers . . . nor powers . . . nor anything else in all creation will be able to separate us from the love of God in Christ Jesus our Lord.'

It wasn't until a few days after I'd met Mordechai that I began to appreciate why he's so hated by many in Israel. I was in Tel Aviv to meet a hugely impressive man called Roni. His eldest son was killed by a suicide bomber and his youngest son took his own life while serving with the army in Gaza. Roni lives with a pain that, please God, I will never imagine. Yet he spoke only of the futility of the 'animal wheel of revenge' and of the need to renounce violence. It was a great privilege to meet him.

At the end of the meeting, encouraged by his talk of non-violence, I mentioned that I had met Mordechai Vanunu. The atmosphere turned icy. People like me, people who live in comfortable Britain, just don't realize the fundamental threat that someone like Vanunu poses to the existence of Israel, he insisted. I have no idea what it is like to live with the fear of being invaded by hostile neighbours or being blown up on a bus. And Roni was right – I don't.

Yet I can find nothing cheap about Vanunu's commitment to non-violence. Christ called his followers to turn the other cheek and became an enemy of the state. His was not a religion of pious respectability, it was a faith that invited derision and scorn. Mordechai continues to pay a heavy price for his Christian pacifism. He has made himself an enemy of the state, remains under house arrest in the cathedral close and is branded a traitor even by his family.

But Roni's point is that it's always others who will pay the real price for Vanunu's pacifism. And this is the hardest of all dilemmas for those who thirst for peace. I suspect it's something even Vanunu continues to wrestle with in the quiet spaces of the cathedral.

The wall makes new Naboths

Church Times, 30 July 2004

Liberation theology may no longer be intellectually fashionable, but who cares about fashion? It provided a theological narrative for those in South America and South Africa around which to rally against the oppression of despotic governments. Yet it cannot work for Palestinians.

The biblical roots of liberation theology are in the Exodus, and the search for a promised land free from Egyptian domination. Therein lies the rub. Although in South America it was a metaphor for freedom, for Palestinians this is the very story that holds them captive. Taken literally, the land is promised by God to the people of Israel. Who cares about the UN and the International Court of Justice when the Bible is your trust deed?

Palestinian Christians need a different paradigm, and find it in the story of Naboth's vineyard. King Ahab wishes to purchase Naboth's vineyard for a vegetable garden. Naboth, however, refuses to sell. In order to gain possession of the land, Ahab's wife concocts a plan to accuse Naboth of blasphemy, for which he is then stoned. Read from this perspective, 1 Kings 21.19 has terrifying relevance: 'Thus says the Lord: in the place where dogs licked up the blood of Naboth, dogs will also lick up your blood.'

Reading the Bible in the shadow of the wall that the Israeli government is erecting throughout Palestinian territory makes one doubly aware how much of the Hebrew Scriptures relates to the theology of land.

The problem with the wall is not the wall per se. The Israelis are entitled to a means of protecting themselves from suicide bombers. For that purpose, it has been extremely successful. Moreover, the idea that walls are of themselves an expression of oppression is not the case: countries are entitled to secure borders.

The problem with the wall is where it actually goes. In many places, it is nowhere near the internationally agreed border between Israel and the West Bank – the so-called green line. Instead, the wall is a de facto land-grab, designed to take in illegally built settlements deep within Palestinian territory.

In many places, the wall separates latter-day Naboths from their vineyards and olive groves. In Qalqiliya, the wall completely surrounds the town, with catastrophic consequences. A GP there gave me a harrowing account of the pregnant women who are stuck for hours at the checkpoint during labour, trying to get to hospital in Nablus. Their children die waiting for Israeli soldiers to process their papers. Nothing good can ever come of this.

Football in Rafah

The *Guardian*, 11 October 2004

At the Sunrise and Hope children's centre, next to the refugee camp in Khan Yunis, I found myself a game. Dozens of small boys gathered for an impromptu replay of England v. France. Amid the ubiquitous graffiti celebrating the heroes of the intifada, we spoke the globalized language of football. 'Zidane, Zidane, he is Arab,' they chuckled. Afterwards, they showed me their burns and bullet wounds, proud of the scars that marked them out as mini-martyrs in the fight against oppression.

But the bravado of the football field was just that. A nurse from the mother and baby clinic in the rabbit-warren Darraj district of Gaza City, where more than 10,000 families are registered, spoke of how all the children suffer bed-wetting and nightmares. Many are too afraid to sleep alone.

The Gaza community mental health programme has catalogued a full range of post-traumatic stress symptoms displayed by the children: stammering, depression, headaches, stomach pains, the inability to concentrate. Behind the cheeky grins, the shooting and shelling is educating the children of Gaza on a daily syllabus of fear.

Pent-up frustration leads to hyperactivity in school. The centre holds daily anger-management classes. For an hour before school the children throw balls against a wall. In the last few years, academic results have plummeted.

It is little wonder. Wella was shot by a sniper during lessons. Unlike the boys, she was close to tears as she showed us a six-inch wound in the centre of her stomach. 'Every time I have a bath I remember when I was injured. I am angry with the soldiers. Why did they do this? I didn't do anything. I was in school.'

Hamas won't need to teach these kids how to graduate from throwing balls to throwing stones and bombs; they are learning all they need to learn about violence from the Israeli Defence Force.

All the children have their stories. Leaa Hussein Najim is 10. 'At 7.30 in the morning the Israeli bulldozers started destroying our house fence. The walls started falling. Big rocks fell down on my leg and it was injured. I was not able to stand on it. My mother carried me while my father carried my grandmother, but he fell down because he was in a hurry. Afterwards I went back. I didn't know where our house was. Everything was under destruction, my books and uniforms.'

Aya Al-Shaer is 13. 'We felt very afraid. My father said to the bulldozer: "Please give me time to take our furniture out of the house." But the bulldozer didn't agree, and started shooting at my father. He was shot in the back and the leg.'

The stories go on. Rouan said she 'sleeps with tears every night'. Another boy from the Brazil area of Rafah returned to search out his clothes and books among the rubble. Finding nothing, he went to school in his pyjamas.

A few hundred yards from six-storey concrete flats, along the ironically named Philadelphi road, a huge Israeli barrier spreads its concrete wings along the length of Rafah. We picked our way through the chewed-up wreckage created by tanks and bull-dozers.

And then, out of nowhere, without us having crossed any sort of line and with no warning, a machine gun from the nearest watchtower opened fire. As we dropped to the ground and scattered, a woman in a nearby tenement continued to hang out her washing. She had seen it all before.

Despite all this, children continue to play. The Gaza strip is one of the most densely populated places on the planet and the majority of the population is under 16. The local zoo may have been destroyed, the football field is far too dangerous, and the beach has been appropriated by settlers and soldiers. Some play football in the cemetery. In Gaza, death is never very far away.

Dear Lord and Father of us all

Thought for the Day, 1 October 2005

I have a bit of a problem with the well-loved hymn, 'Dear Lord and Father of mankind'. On the surface it's a rather engaging hymn about peace – 'drop thy still dews of quietness, till all our strivings cease'. The hymn transports the imagination of the singer to the beautiful shores of the Sea of Galilee: 'O Sabbath rest by Galilee! O calm of hills above.'

But if you stand by the shores of the sea of Galilee you'll realize that the 'hills above' are, in fact, the Golan Heights, and that they are littered with burnt-out tanks and bristling with military bunkers. Many Christian pilgrimages to Galilee take the prayerful to its shores to enjoy the tranquillity, while close by the city of Jenin is little more than rubble and suicide bombers continue to find innocent targets in Tel Aviv and Netanya.

Which brings me to an important distinction – peace can mean two things. It can mean peace and quiet, the absence of noise and hassle – 'drop thy still dews of quietness'. Or it can mean peace as in people not killing each other.

Too often, we think about peace as some sort of mental spa amid life's traumas. After all, most of us want a quiet, hassle-free life. But the process of bringing years of hatred and violent conflict to an end can never be like that. Reconciliation is a frustrating and deeply aggravating business.

Earlier this week, General John de Chastelain and his team announced that they believed the IRA had put all their weapons out of use. Somewhere, somewhen, tons of Semtex and machine guns were disposed of for ever. There was no fanfare or dancing in the street; too many people have lost their lives for that to have been appropriate. Moreover, after years of deception and mistrust on all sides, some find it hard to take this announcement at face value. Is there some clever conspiracy? Are we being manipulated?

It took seven years after the Good Friday agreement, seven years of long meetings and setbacks, seven years of broken promises and tantrums, to reach this point. The search for peace is physically and emotionally exhausting. And if this really is the end, then there doesn't seem to be any great emotional pay-off either.

It's easy to see why people prefer peace to mean some sort of holiday from horrors of the real world. The sort of peace I've described sounds too much like the battle itself. But remember: Jesus said blessed are the peacemakers, not blessed are the peaceful. In a world of almost continual violence, peace and quiet is more a spiritual luxury than a theological and humanitarian necessity. Which is why the bit of the hymn that most resonates with me is the first line: 'Dear Lord and Father of mankind, forgive our foolish ways.'

Chapter 10

Cowboys

Never trust a Christian cowboy

The *Guardian*, 23 October 2002

'I've always acted alone. Americans admire that immensely. Americans like the cowboy who leads the wagon train by riding ahead alone.' So said Henry Kissinger. And he's right. The cowboy represents a popular point of reference in American culture and has been drawn upon by successive US politicians to justify both domestic and foreign policy.

Likewise, war itself is often viewed through the prism of the movie cowboy mythology. Vietnam was described by American troops as 'Indian country'. George Bush even initiated the war on terrorism by declaring he wanted Osama bin Laden 'dead or alive'. Now the focus has turned to Iraq Bush has once again returned to a familiar script. Saddam is an 'outlaw', says Bush; an 'international outlaw', echoes Blair.

Here is the plot of an archetypal western movie: the hero comes to town, though the community does not fully accept him. Some evil threatens to overwhelm the town. Initially, the hero tries to avoid getting involved. However, after exercising much restraint and so as to protect the community, the hero is forced to square up to the villains. Gun in hand, and at considerable personal risk, the hero kills the villains and makes the town safe. The hero leaves town.

This is the paradigm against which war against Saddam is being considered. From Bush's perspective, the resistance of the international community to the war on Iraq is therefore to be expected – it's part of the script. So too, perhaps, is Bush's notorious inarticulacy. For the cowboy is essentially a man of action, not talk. 'So self-contained is the later western hero that he seems to exist beyond the everyday commonplaces of talk and explanation, of persuasion, argument, indeed beyond conversation altogether,' writes Princeton academic and western expert Lee Clark Mitchell.

The image of the lone gunfighter who is suspicious of fancy talk and who acts fearlessly to defeat the forces of evil is the defining mark of a certain sort of US national pride. Some have argued that this pattern exemplifies a sort of redeemer myth. The hero is saviour to the town – thus the cowboy's violence is justified. For in the absence of the rule of law, or in a town where the sheriff is seen as weak (here we see the part assigned to the UN), the cowboy must carry the responsibility for defeating evil.

Bush seems to believe that this cowboy justification for war is also a Christian rationale for war. It isn't. For the cowboy film represents the development of a distinctive ethical stance that is defined in the strongest possible contrast to that of Christianity. 'The meek ain't goin' to inherit nothin' west of Chicago,' said Conn Vallian in *The Quick and the Dead*. In this cowboy film, Christianity is depicted as weak and ineffectual, something commonly practised by women and wholly incapable of dealing with the challenges of the frontier. In *High Noon* Grace Kelly begs Gary Cooper not to take up his gun and face the Miller Gang, but he ignores her Quaker principles. In order to create a safer future for them both he must return to unfinished business and kill the enemy. For the cowboy any sort of Christian forgiveness is never an option. Redemption only comes through violence.

Simon Schama has argued that there is a suffocating 'reverend togetherness' about the US reaction to 9/11 that blocks out the important but awkward questions. This is true, though it suppresses far more than the 'secular debate about liberty'. Theological debate is also stifled. Even in this context of apparent piety would it be possible to imagine a public discussion of how Jesus's instruction to love one's enemies might have political application? Of course not. What is suffocating is the religion of the flag – not the religion of the cross or the crescent. Ironically, it is precisely the desire to be ecumenical and sensitive to all faiths that makes religion easier to conscript as a support for war. For in abstracting out the particular message of each faith tradition in the name of a blanket religiousness, the resistance to war that is differently coded within each faith tradition is effectively neutralized. Once this has been established, religious language and imagery can be applied in support of all sorts of dubious moral purposes.

And that is exactly what is happening at the moment. It is simply that 'reverend togetherness' and the language of 'evil', like the invocation of the western movie script, is employed to solicit maximum justification for the cowboy's course of action.

However, there are other scripts to follow. Sam Peckinpah's 1969 groundbreaking *The Wild Bunch* provides an ominous reductio ad absurdum of the traditional western format. The heroes are thieves who get involved in the politics of another country simply for their own gain. The end is not safety but carnage. 'Peckinpah's shrewdest insight lay in recognizing how essential to the western a form of moral self-deception has always been,' writes Lee Clarke Mitchell. Cowboy ethics always leads to death.

Why I hate Superman

Thought for the Day, 13 July 2006

He came from the stars, wrapped in swaddling clothes, on a mission to save humanity. His foster parents were originally called Mary and Joseph, simple ordinary folk living in the country. But his real father was Jor-El – El being the Hebrew word for God. 'They can be a great people', said Jor-El. 'For this reason I have sent them you, my only son.' And so he took on the likeness of human form, going about among mortals performing miracles, great acts of power. His arch-adversary goes by the name of Lex Luthor – which sounds a lot like Lucifer to me. And his death made the best-selling comic story-line of all time. A devoted female companion discovers the impossible. 'Oh Lord! It's empty! His tomb is empty!' screams an astonished Lois Lane. And sure enough, the half-man, half-God has been resurrected, thus to ascend into the heavens. Little wonder the director of *Superman Returns* – on general release from tomorrow – has called him 'the Jesus Christ of Superheroes'.

So why is it that I can't stand Superman?

For one thing, I dislike all that clean-cut boy scout moralizing. Truth, justice and the American way. Those piercing blue eyes are so reminiscent of the Jesus stereotype made famous by Robert Powell. In Superman, virtue is depicted as good-looking yet sexually inert. Jesus becomes the wholesome hero of Smallville, USA.

More troubling still is the one-dimensional moral universe that Superman inhabits. It's a place where the goodies look like goodies and the baddies like baddies, designed to sell the comforting idea that in the great battle of good and evil, it's easy to tell who's who. The early Church called it Gnosticism, and dismissed it as the first great heresy.

For the Church has always maintained that Jesus is fully and completely human. And furthermore, that the salvation of the world is bound up with God sharing our humanity. Christians take this to mean that tragic, ugly, dysfunctional reality is to be recycled from within the human condition. Salvation is a transformation of what it is to be human, not something that just happens to us by some alien power.

For in reality, we are all complicated alloys of generous and corrupt, selfish and compassionate, peaceful and cruel. Human beings are capable of great sacrifice and tenderness, as well as the monstrous brutality of planting bombs on trains.

Superman is a refusal to accept that we are complicated creatures. It's a fantasy of salvation without the painful rigours of self-knowledge, presuming that salvation is achieved when the goodies have destroyed the baddies. The problem is: I don't know which one of those is me.

Gunfighter cool

Church Times, 22 August 2003

Often I have students who think that the best way to demonstrate intelligence is to exhibit an air of disdainful superiority towards the great thinkers of the past. Dismissing Aquinas or Hegel with some snappy put-down has become the mark of a sort of academic cool. To be clever is to be uncommitted and sceptical.

These same students find it impossible to defend any intellectual territory of their own. Taking up a position makes them vulnerable to the same hit-and-run cleverness too often prized by the academy.

A profound, if unlikely, commentary on this condition was offered on television recently in the form of the classic western of 1961, *The Magnificent Seven*. Though the film purists prefer Kurosawa's *The Seven Samurai*, and my children opt for *A Bug's Life*, the Disney remake, *The Magnificent Seven* is much more than a simple cowboy film – it's a critique of what it is to be cool.

The film's fundamental contrast is between the life of the gunfighter and that of the farmer. The gunfighters, led by Yul Brynner and Steve McQueen, are quintessentially cool. They are drifters with no responsibilities, no ties, no family or home. Their deadpan expressions betray nothing that might disrupt their studied self-sufficiency.

The farmers, on the other hand, are deeply uncool. The nature of their occupation ties them to a particular location. Growing corn means defending territory; it is a commitment that renders them vulnerable (in this case, to bandits). Yet it is only when territory is defended that space is created to find love, have a family, and care for the sick and elderly.

Having fallen in love with one of the village girls, the novice gunman played by Horst Buchholz is forced to choose: settle down, or ride into the sunset. Despite the fact that Buchholz's character has always been desperate for gunfighter cool, he gives it up for love. Before the end credits roll, he takes off his gunbelt and settles down with his new girlfriend to strip the corn.

Appropriately, at the centre of the farmers' village lies the church. Like the village, the Church accepts vulnerability as the price paid for defending territory. Like the village, the Church is often uncool. Frequently its critics have the best of the argument. Yet the only way to be safe is to believe in nothing much at all – like the mercenary gunfighters or my supercool students. However difficult it is to defend, the Church continues to mark out a space to live and love and grow. However fragile, it is a space we will always need.